An experiment on the surface of the Moon. Col. Edwin E. Aldrin stands beside the apparatus for measuring Solar Wind which was erected soon after the Apollo 11 landing on July 20, 1969. The lunar module stands in the background. See article on the Moon in this volume.

HARVER
JUNIOR WORLD
ENCYCLOPEDIA

Michael W. Dempsey B.A.

Harver Educational Services, Inc. • Freeport, N.Y. • Toronto, Canada

Over Four Thousand Million Years Ago

Consultant Advisory Board

Sir Bernard Lovell
O.B.E., L.L.D., D.SC., F.R.S.
Professor of Radio Astronomy
in the University of
Manchester. Director of the
Nuffield Radio Astronomy
Laboratories, Jodrell Bank

Maurice Burton D.SC.
Naturalist and Author
Joint General Editor of
Animal Life encyclopedia

Yehudi Menuhin K.B.E.
Violinist
Winner of the 1968 Nehru
Award for the Furthering
of Human Relations and
International Understanding

Professor Asa Briggs M.A.
Historian
Vice-Chancellor of the
University of Sussex,
England

Editorial Advisory Board

Michael Chinery B.A.
Trevor Marchington M.A.

Lionel Munby M.A.
Tony Osman M.SC., A.R.C.S.

Planning Editor

Burton Lasky B.A.

Editorial Board

Editor-in-Chief
Michael W. Dempsey B.A.

Executive Editors
Philip M. Clark B.A.
Angela Sheehan B.A.

Art Editor
Derek Aslett

Production Controller
Stephen Pawley

Production Editor
Sarah Tyzack

Picture Researchers
Marian Gain
Belinda Siddeley

© B.P.C. PUBLISHING LIMITED, 1972
LIBRARY OF CONGRESS CATALOG CARD NUMBER 70-127806

Made and printed in Great Britain by Purnell
and Sons Ltd, Paulton (Somerset) and London

The Evolution of the Earth.

500,000,000 Years Ago

Present Day

Contributors

Neil Ardley B.SC.
A. L. Barrett
N. S. Barrett M.A.
Paul Bendix B.A.
Carole Berkson
Lucy Berman B.A.
A. S. Butterfield
Rita Carter
Ronald L. Carter B.SC.
Ann Clark
John O. E. Clark B.SC.
J. N. Cleaver M.A.
T. G. Cook M.A.
Jean Cooke
Heather Dean B.A.
Jill R. Girling B.A.
Peter Grey
Lionel Grigson M.A.
R. J. W. Hammond
Brendan Hennessy
L. James M.A. PH.D.
Robin Kerrod
Ann Kramer
Jo Logan
K. E. Lowther M.A.
Keith Lye B.A., F.R.G.S.
Patricia Miller B.A.
Peter Muccini M.A.
L. H. Munby M.A.
Ruth Petrie B.A.
Dominic Recaldin B.SC., PH.D.
G. E. Satterthwaite
D. S. Sehbai M.A.
D. Sharp L.R.A.M.
Martin Stoll B.A.
Elena Trevino A.A.
Marie Weinstein B.A.
G. M. Weston B.A.
B. G. Wilson
Michael E. Wright B.A.
Jade Zurek

Monarchy is a system of government under which a country is governed by one ruler, usually for his or her lifetime. Until the late 1700's, most countries were governed by monarchs. Monarchs had titles such as emperor, king, prince, sultan or tsar. In some countries monarchs were elected. Today many countries of the world are republics. Most countries that are not republics are *constitutional* monarchies, where the real power is held by elected governments and where the monarch is head of state but not head of the government.

Monarchs usually inherited their titles and thrones from their fathers or other royal relatives. In some countries, women could inherit thrones to become empresses, queens or tsarinas. In other countries women monarchs were not allowed. When women monarchs have come to the throne, they have often been very forceful rulers, such as Cleopatra of Egypt, Queen Elizabeth I of England or Empress Catherine the Great of Russia.

In earliest times, monarchs were military leaders and usually the most powerful fighters. For example, most of the kings mentioned in the Bible relied on their ability as generals to keep their position as kings. The same was true in Ancient Greece. Alexander the Great of Macedonia was a brilliant general, and at the end of his reign his empire stretched from Greece to India. Many early kings were regarded as priests or holy men. The pharaohs of Egypt were even thought to be living gods. Later, the Greek and Roman kings and emperors were sometimes worshipped as gods. In the Middle Ages, in Europe, people thought that kings were chosen by God, and the kings were crowned and blessed by bishops. Many thought that these kings had special power to heal the sick. There was even a disease (scrofula) called 'King's Evil'. It was thought that a sick person could only be cured of this illness if the king touched him.

In England in the 1700's, King Charles I

Louis XIV of France, the 'Sun King', the longest reigning monarch in European history, ruled from 1643 to 1715.

PRESENT DAY MONARCHS

European Monarchs

Country	Monarch	Came to Throne
Belgium	King Baudouin	1951
Denmark	King Frederick IX	1947
Great Britain*	Queen Elizabeth II	1952
Liechtenstein	Prince Franz Josef II	1938
Luxembourg	Grand Duke Jean	1964
Monaco	Prince Rainier III	1949
Netherlands	Queen Juliana	1948
Norway	King Olav V	1957
Sweden	King Gustav VI Adolf	1950

Asian Monarchs

Afghanistan	King Zahir Shah	1933
Bahrain	Sheikh Isa bin Sulman Al Khalifah	1961
Bhutan	King Jigme Dorji Wangchuk	1952
Brunei	Sultan Hassanal	1967
Iran	Shah Mohammed Reza Pahlavi	1941
Japan	Emperor Hirohito	1926
Jordan	King Hussein	1952
Kuwait	Sheikh Sabah as-Salim as-Sabah	1965
Laos	King Savang Vatthana	1959
Muscat and Oman	Sultan Said bin Taimur	1932
Nepal	King Mahendra	1955
Qatar	Sheikh Ahmad	1960
Saudi Arabia	King Faisal	1964
Sikkim	Chogyal Palden Thondup Namgyal	1963
Thailand	King Bhumibol	1946
Trucial States	Seven sheikhs	

African Monarchs

Ethiopia	Emperor Haile Selassie I	1930
Morocco	King Hassan II	1961
Swaziland	King Sobhuza II	1967

Pacific Island Monarch

Tonga	King Taufa'ahau Tupou IV	1965

* The monarch of Great Britain is independently the monarch of Australia, Barbados, Canada, Ceylon, Gambia, Guyana, Jamaica, Malta, Mauritius, New Zealand, Sierra Leone and Trinidad-Tobago. These countries are independent members of the British Commonwealth.

believed that he ruled by *divine right* — that is, he thought that God had appointed him king and that he was responsible only to God for his actions. The English parliament did not accept this idea. They accused Charles of being an *absolutist* monarch, who wanted complete power for himself. In 1648, after a civil war, Parliament had Charles executed (see Civil War, English).

From the late 1700's, people began to attack the idea of monarchies. In 1775, thirteen colonies in America broke away from Britain and its monarch George III. The United States did not choose a king; instead, it became the first modern republic. In 1789, the French Revolution resulted in the fall of the French King Louis XVI and his execution.

Many European monarchies collapsed as a result of World War I (1914-18) and World War II (1939-45). Many nations no longer wanted monarchies, and replaced them with republics. Republics were regarded as more democratic than monarchies, as presidents were usually elected.

Above: The Monastery of the Cross, Israel.
Left: The Monastery of Hosias Loukas in Greece.

Whether situated in isolation or otherwise, monasteries tend to be more or less self-sufficient communities. The word monastery comes from Greek, and means 'living alone'.

Dates When Some Important Monarchies Collapsed

1792	After the Revolution, of 1789, France set up its first republic.
1889	Monarchy came to an end in Brazil.
1911	China ceased to be a monarchy.
1917	Russian revolutionaries overthrew the Tsar.
1918	The German and Austro-Hungarian monarchies collapsed at the end of World War I.
1946	Following World War II, Italy became a republic.

Monasteries are places in which monks live in a religious community governed by strict rules of conduct. Monasteries play an important part in Christianity, Buddhism, and Jainism. In Burma and Thailand most young men become monks for at least a short time and then go back to their normal jobs. But many Christian monasteries are closed communities in which the monks have little contact with the outside world or indeed, in some cases, with each other.

Most religious *orders* (groups) have strict rules. Buddhist monks observe more than two hundred rules. Among them are rules that monks may not take life, steal, eat or drink too much, sleep in luxury, or possess gold and silver. Most Christian orders have three main rules known as the Counsels of Perfection. The monks vow to live in obedience, poverty, and chastity. They spend the day in prayer and work either in the monastery or outside it.

Most monasteries depend on the gifts of religious people. Some monks actually beg for food and money. Many Buddhist monks go around with begging bowls. The Christian Dominicans and Franciscans are also *mendicant* (begging) orders. But most monasteries support themselves to some extent by selling farm produce, wine, perfume, or carvings in addition to general souvenirs.

Christian monastic life probably originated in Egypt in the 200's, when St Anthony brought together a number of hermits into a community with definite rules. In 320 the monk St Pachomius founded the first monastery. In the 360's St Basil of Cappadocia laid down rules that were accepted by many communities. Monastic life has changed little in the Eastern Christian Church. Its center is the group of monasteries at Mount Athos in Greece. No female—human or animal—is allowed there.

Monasteries in the Western Church developed from the ideas of St Benedict, who in the 500's organized monasteries on a system of work, worship, and sleep. In England King Henry VIII abolished most of the monasteries in the 1500's.

Money At one time, when people wanted to buy anything they had to give something else in exchange for it. For example, if a farmer wanted to buy bread from a baker, he offered him eggs in exchange. The baker would accept them because he needed eggs. At this period, a person's 'money' consisted of the goods that he possessed or could produce. As communities became larger and trade developed, this method of buying, called *barter*, appeared to be a clumsy way of carrying on buying and selling. Some people then had the idea of using *token goods* for trade, things that all people considered precious and would accept. In many parts of the world, cattle were used as token goods or *money*. Today, in parts of Africa, they are still considered as the only real wealth. The English word *pecuniary* (consisting of money) comes from the Latin word *pecus*, meaning *cattle*.

The first people who are known to have used coins as money were the Lydians, who lived in Asia Minor. They began using stamped pieces of metal as a *medium of exchange* (that is, for buying and selling) as early as the 7th century B.C. But it is believed that the Chinese may have made coins at an even earlier date than that. The early coins were of irregular shapes and were stamped with rough designs. At one period of history, the Chinese shaped each coin into the form of the article it would buy. For example, the coins used for buying clothes were shaped like the human body.

Until recent times, the *money value* of coins (the amount coins were worth when used as money) depended on the value of the metal that the coins were made of. But today most countries use only *token coins*. This means that the value stamped on a coin is not the same as the value of the metal in the coin.

The economic troubles that followed the First World War led to many changes in people's thinking about money. Governments came to accept that there was no need for coins to be valuable in themselves. All that mattered was their value as money. Most governments began to issue token coins. Almost all the coins that are in circulation today are token coins. Their value as money is not related to the value of the metal of which they are made. People accept a coin in payment not because they value the coin itself but because they have confidence in the authority that issued the coin. Because coins are heavy and bulky, they are chiefly used for making only small pay-

A view of the high altar in the Benedictine monastery of Fischingen, in Switzerland.

Above and left: Ancient Greek coins. *Obverse* (front) and *reverse* (back) of a coin of Mithradates, King of Pontus, about 100 B.C. (above); and of a coin of Alexander the Great, 300's B.C. (left). The custom of showing a ruler or head of government on the obverse of coins has continued to the present day.

Left: Obverse and reverse of a Roman *solidus* of the emperor Constantine III (early A.D. 400's).

The female figure of Britannia, representing Britain, has traditionally appeared on various English coins, such as this one. Such symbolic designs are often used for coins.

Left: An English gold coin of the reign (1625-49) of Charles I.
Right: Early paper money, such as these Russian banknotes of the 1800's, tended to be elaborately ornate.
Below: Two examples of modern coin design.
Below right: A German banknote for 2 million marks. At the end of World War I, inflation in Germany was so great that notes were printed to cover vast sums of money.

ments. Larger payments are made in paper money which is issued by banks authorized to do so by a government.

As banking developed, many people found it more convenient to put their currency (coins and paper money) in a bank. They could then make payments or receive payments by means of checks, and could leave in the bank for safe keeping any money that they did not need immediately. Today, very many people in most countries of the world use the services of a bank in this way. (See Banking.)

Governments control and regulate the use of money. A country's government decides what the basic *unit of currency* in the country will be. It decides what paper money shall be made and circulated, and what kind and value of coins shall be in use. Sometimes, the *nominal value* of a coin or piece of paper money (the value stamped or printed on it) is not the same as its real value. The real value depends on the amount of goods the coin or note will purchase. During times of *inflation*, the real value of money goes down, because it will purchase fewer goods. In times of *deflation* the real value of money tends to rise. Prices tend to reduce and money therefore purchases more goods. Inflation is much more common than deflation.

Mongolia consists of a large plateau in eastern central Asia. Much of it is covered by the Gobi, a cold, bleak, stony desert. Mongolia is divided into two parts. Inner Mongolia is part of China. The rest of the region, once called Outer Mongolia, is now the Mongolian People's Republic.

The country of Mongolia is bordered by the USSR to the north and China to the south. Only 1,091,000 people live in the Mongolian People's Republic's 592,665 square miles Its capital is Ulan Bator. Mongolia lies between about 1,500 and 14,000 feet above sea-level. The country's known mineral resources include coal, copper, gold and iron.

The location map shows the position of the east-central Asian region of Mongolia.

Above: A view of the Arybalu Temple in Ulan Bator, the capital of the Mongolian People's Republic (outer Mongolia). The temple is now disused, but some of its enormous bells are still in place on its terraces. In the temple courtyard, some *yurts* (hide and felt tents) have been set up. Mongolians live in them either by preference or because they are waiting for modern apartments.
Below: A group of nomadic, or wandering, Mongolians. Most Mongolians who live outside the cities work on livestock ranches.

A mass rally in the central square of Ulan Bator, the capital of the Mongolian People's Republic. The city has many modern buildings and a university. Its industries produce woolen textiles, leatherware and meat products

Despite its small population, Mongolia has more than 10 million two-humped camels, cattle, goats and horses, and as many sheep. Until the 1950's most Mongolians were nomads. Today, outside the cities, most Mongolians are now settled on huge government-run ranches.

Mongolia was once the center of a vast empire. In the A.D. 1200's, Mongol tribes united under Ghengis Khan to conquer most of the land between Japan and Europe. The Mongol empire did not last long, however. It later formed part of the Manchu empire, which included China. China finally recognized Mongolia's independence in 1946.

Mongols The greatest nomad attack on civilization was made by the Mongols. In 1206 a Mongol, Temujin, was chosen as Khakhan, or great ruler, at a tribal meeting at Karakorum, near Lake Baikal in Siberia. He took the name Chinghis or Genghiz (the strong) and ordered his followers to conquer the world. By his death in 1227, the Mongols ruled from the Volga river to the north China coast. They were deadly fighters from horseback. With the invention of the bridle and the stirrup, they could use lances and shoot bows when riding. The Mongols killed the peoples they conquered in terrible massacres. They saved and gave power to merchants, artisans and scholars.

Ogodai, Genghiz's third son, became Khakhan and began the conquest of China. To Batu, son of Genghiz Khan's eldest son, had been left the conquest of Europe. This began in 1236 with the help of Subatai, the Mongol cavalry general. In 1240-2 Batu swept through western Russia, Poland, Czechoslovakia and Hungary, defeating all he met. Slav civilization was devastated. When they heard of Ogodai's death the Mongols left Europe to take part in the election of the new

Khakhan. Hulagu, another grandson, conquered Arabia and attacked Egypt in 1255-8. His victories and massacres did an enormous amount of damage to Muslim civilization.

Mangu, the fourth Khakhan, and his brother Kublai conquered southern China in 1257-9. In 1259 Kublai succeeded Mangu as Khakhan and also became Emperor of China. The Mongols had ceased to be nomads. Under Kublai Khan there was peace and order over the whole area between Europe and China; trade in silk flourished. Europe and Asia were brought into contact. (See China; Great Wall of China; Marco Polo; Nomads; Turks.)

Mongoose This is a small flesh-eating animal related to the civet. There are many species (kinds) of mongooses, all of them natives of Africa or the southern half of Asia. They grow to about 1½ feet in length. They have bushy, tapered tails, and long bristly hair.

An Egyptian Mongoose.

Mongooses kill and eat mice, rats, poultry, and other small animals. They are very fond of birds' eggs. They pick these up and throw them down to break them before eating the contents. But mongooses are best known for their ability to kill dangerous poisonous snakes, such as cobras. Their great speed enables them to do this.

Monkeys are furry animals related to the apes (see Apes). Most monkeys are smaller than apes and, unlike apes, generally have long tails. Their arms are shorter in proportion to their legs than are those of apes. Monkeys are less intelligent than apes, but have highly developed brains compared with other animals. They are clever with their hands and feet, and can grasp and hold objects.

Most monkeys live in trees, and are agile at running and leaping through the forests, many feet above the ground. All monkeys but the douroucouli of South America rest at night and are active during the day. The main food of monkeys is fruit and other plant food, insects and other small creatures, and birds' eggs.

Biologists divide monkeys into two major groups. They are the *Old World monkeys* of Africa, Asia and the southwestern tip of Europe, and the *New World monkeys* of Central and South America. They show some striking differences. The Old World monkeys have longer noses, and eyes and nostrils that are closer together. They include a number of ground-dwelling kinds. All New World monkeys, on the other hand, live in trees. Many of them have *prehensile* tails — tails with which they can grip branches and swing along. No Old World monkeys can do this.

The macaques form a large Old World group. They include the common rhesus monkey and the barbary ape of Gibraltar — the only European monkey. The long-snouted baboons form another large group. They often live on the ground in large groups. Other Old World species include the long-nosed proboscis monkey of Borneo, which is a good swimmer, and the colobus monkey, which has long silky fur.

Important groups of New World monkeys include the small titis and sakis; the large, noisy howlers; the capucins, intelligent, acrobatic creatures; and the extremely common squirrel monkeys. The spider monkeys have long limbs, while the woolly monkeys are covered in thick, dark fur. The marmosets include the smallest of all monkeys.

Monroe Doctrine This American policy was announced by President James Monroe in a speech to Congress on December 2, 1823. Monroe stated that the Americas were no longer open to colonization, and that European powers could not interfere in the Western Hemisphere. In turn, the United States would not interfere in European affairs. This policy had, in fact, been stated earlier by presidents Washington and Jefferson, but after Monroe's speech it became known as the Monroe Doctrine.

The policy was announced for several reasons. One was to protect the Latin American countries, which had recently won independence from Spain, from the *Holy Alliance*. This was a powerful alliance formed by Russia, Austria and Prussia. France was also suspected of trying to restore Latin American colonies to Spain. Another motive for announcing the doctrine was to discourage Russia from expanding its territories in Alaska.

The United States was not alone in its fear of the Holy Alliance. Interference with the Latin American countries would have badly affected Britain's trade. The British foreign minister George Canning proposed that Britain and the United States should make a joint declaration to warn off European intrusions. But the United States did not want an alliance with Britain.

The doctrine was mainly ignored until 1865, when France sent troops to conquer Mexico. The United States sent a strong message to France, and the troops were withdrawn. In 1895, the doctrine was again called upon when Britain disputed the boundaries of Venezuela and British Guiana (now Guyana). In 1904, Theodore Roosevelt stated that further interference in Latin America would bring interference from the United States. But later presidents have tended to avoid this harsh policy. In 1962, the United States exerted pressure on the USSR to remove its missiles from Cuba, because they were a direct threat to the Americas.

James Monroe, 5th president (1817-25) of the United States, is best remembered for establishing the 'Monroe Doctrine', which forbade European intervention in the Americas.

Monroe, James (1758-1831), served as 5th president of the United States from 1817 to 1825. One of his most important acts was to establish, together with John Quincy Adams, the 'Monroe Doctrine' (see Monroe Doctrine). The other major issue of Monroe's presidency was whether slavery should be permitted in the new territories of the Midwest. The issue was temporarily settled by the Missouri Compromise of 1820-21. By this, Congress passed bills admitting Maine as a free state and Missouri as a slave state.

Born in Westmoreland County, Virginia, Monroe left college to fight Britain in the War of Independence. From 1790-94 he was a senator. As envoy to France in 1803, he negotiated the Louisiana Purchase. Under President Madison he was secretary of state (1811-17) and secretary of war (1814-15). After his second term as president, Monroe retired to Virginia. He died in New York City.

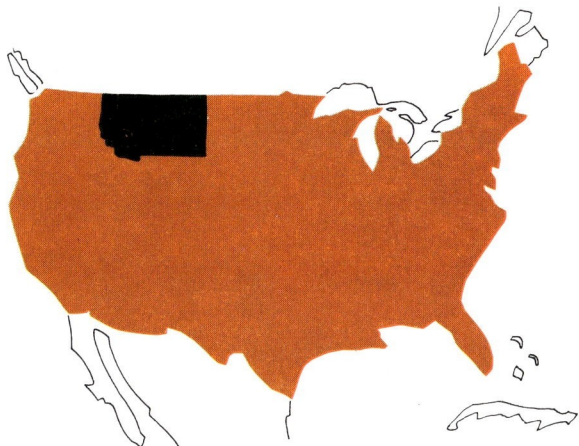

The map shows the location of Montana.

Montana, America's northernmost Rocky Mountain state, lies on the Canadian border between Idaho in the west and the Dakotas in the east. It covers an area of 147,138 square miles. Montana means *mountainous* in Spanish. Montana is also called 'Land of the Shining Mountains' and 'The Big Sky Country'. High rugged mountains cover western Montana, where the highest point is Granite Peak (12,799 feet). Eastwards, the mountains thin out and the land becomes a grassy plain.

About half of Montana's 682,000 people live in rural areas. Only five cities have more than 20,000 people, including Helena, the state capital. Seven Indian tribal reservations lie within the state. The tribes include the Assiniboin and Sioux, Blackfeet, Chippewa-Cree, Salish and Kootenai, Crow, Northern Cheyenne, and the Fort Belknap Indian Community.

Montana's 29,000 farms produce more than half of the state's total income. Wheat, barley, hay and sugar beet are leading crops. But only one-fourth of the farmland is used for crop raising. The poorer soil is grassland where farmers rear large herds of cattle and sheep. Montana is rich in minerals, especially petroleum and natural gas. Most of the state's manufacturing industries are based on its agricultural and mineral resources.

The earliest known inhabitants of Montana were the Indian tribes. French fur trappers were active in the area in the

Montana has beautiful mountain scenery, including the Alpine wildflower meadows in Glacier National Park.

mid-1700's. American fur trappers built the first known permanent settlement in Montana in 1847. By 1864, Montana was created a territory. Indian wars continued until 1877, when a federal army crushed all Indian opposition. Montana prospered as a cattle-raising territory after the Northern Pacific Railroad was opened in 1883. This provided transportation to the great cities in the east. In 1889, Montana became the 41st state. By 1900, the state grew rich from its minerals and its economy boomed in and after World War II.

Montreal is the largest city in Quebec province, Canada, with a population of 1,435,000. It occupies a commanding position at the confluence of the St Lawrence and Ottawa rivers. Villa-Marie, a small settlement of 1642, became a base for traders and explorers. Incorporated as a city in 1832, it has developed into one of the world's most important ports and a chief commercial and industrial center of Canada. It is also a leading educational and cultural center. The port is a hub of the network of ocean and lake traffic through the St Lawrence Seaway which has its entrance in the harbor.

A view of the center of Montreal with the St Lawrence River in the background.

Moon As the Earth travels around the Sun, it is accompanied by its nearest neighbor in space, the Moon. The Moon is called the Earth's *satellite*, and revolves around the Earth in a definite, regular path called the Moon's *orbit*.

The Moon is held in its orbit by the *gravitational attraction* of the Earth. This was first explained by the great scientist Sir Isaac Newton (1642-1727). He knew that every object attracted every other object. He explained how this force of attraction (the *force of gravity*) keeps the planets revolving in their orbits around the Sun and the Moon in its orbit around the Earth.

The Moon is about a quarter the size of the Earth in diameter, and its weight is about one-eightieth that of the Earth. Astronomers know a great deal about the Moon. It is bleak, and has no air or water. It has a hard surface, partly covered with dust and pitted with craters. It has great, dry plains, known as *maria*, or *seas*, and towering, jagged mountains. On the Moon, days are extremely hot and nights extremely cold. In the 1960's, our knowledge of the Moon greatly increased. Space probes and manned flights brought back much information. On July 20, 1969, Neil Armstrong and Edwin Aldrin were the first men to walk on the Moon. They and the astronauts of Apollo 12, which landed on the Moon on November 19, 1969, brought back samples of rocks which showed that the Moon is probably as old as the Earth. The danger of manned flights to the Moon was, however, demonstrated in April 1970 when Apollo 13 was forced to abandon a landing after an explosion in the service module.

The Moon's orbit round the Earth is not quite circular. It is *elliptical* (oval). As a result, the Moon is nearer the Earth at some times than it is at others. When the Moon is near the Earth, it travels faster along its orbit than when it is farther away. Its average speed is about 2,300 miles an hour.

The average distance of the Moon from the Earth is about 239,000 miles. In space, this is a short distance. A rocket that took a day to travel from the Earth to the Moon, would take a year to reach the Sun, traveling at the same speed.

Because the Moon is near the Earth, it appears to us to be much bigger than the stars. In fact, the stars and all the planets are bigger than the Moon, some of them millions of times bigger.

The Moon takes 27 days and 8 hours to travel around the Earth. It also takes exactly the same time to rotate once upon its own axis. As a result, the same part of the Moon's surface is always turned towards the Earth. Our first knowledge of what the other side of the Moon looks like came in 1959 when the Russian space-probe Lunik 3 transmitted photographs of the hidden side back to Earth. All of the Moon has now been mapped by lunar orbiter probes. Apart from the great Mare Orientalis, the far side of the Moon lacks the maria that are a feature of the side we can see.

The Moon has no light of its own. The silvery moonlight which has inspired poets, painters, and musicians, is really light from the Sun which is reflected by the Moon's surface.

As the Moon moves around the Earth, different portions of its surface receive the sunlight. This causes it to appear to us almost as though the Moon changes its shape as the month goes on. We call these 'changes' the *phases* of the Moon. The phases range from New Moon (when the Moon is not visible at all), through First Quarter (half illuminated) to Full Moon (whole disc illuminated). From Full Moon the sunlit part of the disc turned towards us gradually shrinks, through Last Quarter (half illuminated) to New Moon again.

The craters or ring formations on the Moon's surface range from vast mountain-encircled plains, up to 150 miles across, to tiny pits only two or three feet across.

The largest craters can be seen with good binoculars, but the smallest crater

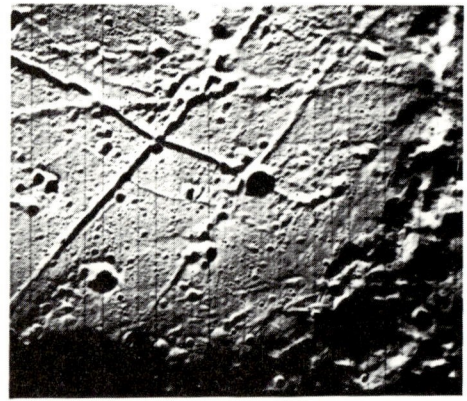

The Moon

Above left: A photograph of the crater Langrenus from the Apollo 8 spacecraft. This crater is 85 miles in diameter.

Above right: A mosaic of the lunar landscape built up from photographs taken by Surveyor 3 which landed in the Ocean of Storms.

Right: The floor of the crater Hevelius, seen from Lunar Orbiter 3. This picture was taken from an altitude of about 36 miles.

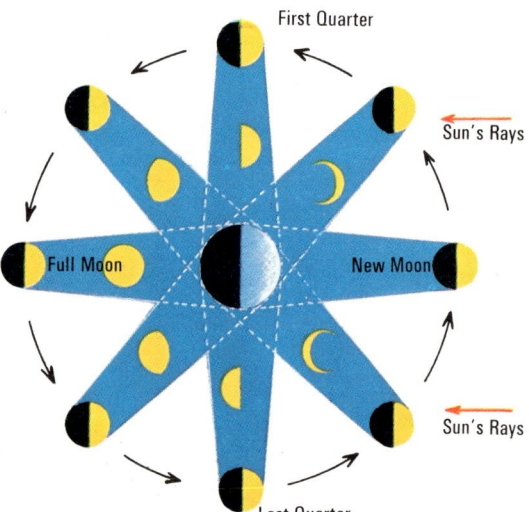

Above: Phases of the Moon. We only see the part of the Moon which is illuminated by the Sun. When the Moon is between the Earth and the Sun none of the illuminated side can be seen from the Earth (new Moon). When the Moon is at the other side of the Earth the whole of the illuminated side can be seen (full Moon). Between these two positions we see part of the illuminated side.

Right: What the Earth looks like from the Moon. In the foreground is the Moon's barren surface. The surface of the Earth is obscured by a layer of cloud. This photograph was taken from Apollo 8.

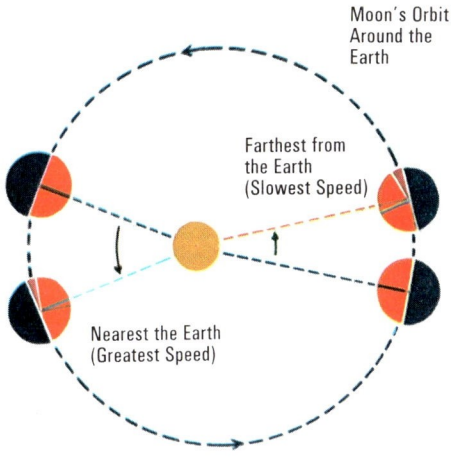

Owing to its slight wobbling movement it is possible to see around alternate 'edges' of the Moon.

The side of the Moon which faces the Earth.

This picture of the far side of the Moon is based on photographs taken by the Russian automatic interplanetary station, Lunik 3.

pits can be detected only on the photographs brought back by astronauts or transmitted back by space probes.

Some of the craters have bright streaks radiating from them called *ray systems*. These can be seen most easily at Full Moon. Astronomers do not know what causes them.

The great plains *(maria)* have very few large craters, and are dark in color compared with the mountainous areas.

Mormons This is the common name for members of the Church of Jesus Christ of Latter-Day Saints. This church was founded in 1830 in the United States by Joseph Smith (1805-44). He claimed that in 1827 he had discovered new religious scriptures called the 'Book of Mormon' near Palmyra, New York. Smith gained many converts, and Mormon settlements were soon established in Missouri. However, the Mormons' customs caused conflict with their neighbors, and in 1838-9, they were expelled from Missouri. They then settled in Nauvoo, Illinois, but in 1844, Smith and his brother were killed by a mob. In 1847, the Mormons, under their new leader Brigham Young (1801-77), went to Great Salt Lake Valley, in present-day Utah, where they founded Salt Lake City. In 1850, Congress recognized the area as the territory of Utah. However, Congress refused to grant statehood to Utah because of the Mormon doctrine of *polygamy* (having many wives). In 1890, the Mormons gave up polygamy, and in 1896, Utah was admitted to the Union.

Morocco is a Muslim kingdom in the extreme north-west of Africa inhabited mostly by Arabs and Berbers. Many French, Spanish and Jewish people also live there.

The country has long, temperate Mediterranean and Atlantic coastlines. But the land merges southwards and eastwards into the barren Sahara desert. The snow-capped Atlas Mountains straddle the country from north-east to south-west. Several rivers flow through semi-desert areas, creating fertile valleys and oases where many farmers have settled.

Morocco has a pleasant climate which is less extreme than most other African countries. Rainfall is moderate, but sufficient to make much of the country suitable for crops or for pasture land. Most Moroccans are farmers.

Many Moroccans still wear flowing robes as their ancestors did, and most Arab women wear the veil. Arabic is the main language, but Berber, French and Spanish are widely spoken.

Once under Carthaginian and Roman rule, Morocco fell to Arab armies in the A.D. 600's. From the 1300's to the 1800's, ferocious Moroccan pirates were widely feared by seamen.

In 1912, France took most of Morocco. Spain took the northern Mediterranean strip, and the port of Tangier was put under international control. Morocco gained complete independence in 1956. At the end of 1968, Spain ceded its tiny colony of Ifni, which it had ruled for 35 years, to Morocco.

In Salt Lake City, Utah, a group of Mormon missionaries receive last instructions before leaving to travel to many parts of the world. Mormons remain an active religious group today.

Morse code is a method of sending messages by telegraph, by radio, or even by light signals. It consists of a series of dots and dashes to represent letters, numbers and punctuation marks. Letters are represented by up to four dots and dashes. Numbers consist of five dots and dashes, and the punctuation marks are made up of six. One dot represents E and one dash T, the letters that occur most often in English. Morse code was invented in the United States in 1840 by Samuel Morse (1791-1872), who also invented the telegraph. Morse code became an international code, used for telegraph and news messages around the world.

Morse code was useful because it is easier to send a message by telegraph or radio consisting only of short or long bursts of power, than to send an actual voice. Nowadays telegraph messages are sent by automatic *teleprinting* machines. Army signalmen still use Morse code and Morse code messages are sent between ships by flashing a light. The code is sometimes used for sending telegrams.

A portrait of Samuel Morse, the inventor of Morse code. The portrait is reproduced from an early photograph by Louis Daguerre, inventor of the *daguerreotype* process.

Mosaic is a form of decoration built up from small pieces of colored glass, stone, china, or other material. The pieces are set in cement. *Grout*, another kind of cement, is used to fill the cracks between them. Mosaic is used mostly on floors, walls, and table tops. It can easily be cleaned by washing, and is extremely hard

Facts and Figures
Area: 171,834 square miles.
Population: 14,300,000.
Capital: Rabat.

Above: A Mosque in Marrakesh, the second largest city in Morocco.
Above right: Pottery merchants in Tangiers.
Left: The map shows the location (marked in black) of Morocco.
Right: Berber women. Berbers make up about a quarter of the population of Morocco.

wearing. Many mosaic floors made by Greeks and Romans nearly 2,000 years ago still exist. Mosaic is laid either in one color or in a combination of colors forming a pattern. Many fine mosaics are laid in the form of pictures.

Moscow is the capital city of Russia. It is situated on the Moskva River in the European portion of the Russian Socialist Federal Soviet Republic (R.S.F.S.R.) the largest of the 15 constituent republics

A fine mosaic in the Basilica of San Vitale at Ravenna, Italy. It portrays Christ among the archangels.

The Church of St. Basil, in Moscow, stands on the south side of Red Square.

of the U.S.S.R. It was made the capital of the Soviet Union in 1918 when the seat of government was removed from Leningrad. With a population of 6,567,000, it is the largest city in Russia and the sixth largest city in the world. It is a picturesque city of many gilded domes, broad avenues and spacious squares.

Moscow is the country's political and administrative center. The city is built on and around the site of the *Kremlin,* the ancient walled citadel or acropolis.

The Kremlin is the seat of the highest state bodies of the Soviet Union, the Supreme Soviet (Parliament) and the Council of Ministers. Within the walls are palaces, cathedrals and offices. The Uspenski Cathedral was the crowning place of the tsars, and the Arkhangelski their place of burial.

The city is the chief financial and business center. It is a hub of rail and waterborne traffic with considerable European and Asian trade. As the major trading center it has extensive steel and textile interests and many factories producing cotton, wool, silk and leather goods.

Moscow is a great seat of learning with many schools of varying grades. The Lomonosov University, the State University, on the Lenin Hills is the largest higher education establishment in Russia. The U.S.S.R. Academy of Sciences and many other academies provide specialized training.

The city is also an important cultural center with large museums, public libraries, concert halls and drama theaters with rich and varied repertoires. In the world of music and drama, the fame of the Bolshoi Theater and Ballet, the State Symphony Orchestra of the U.S.S.R., and the State Folk Dance Company is renowned.

Mosquito The mosquito is a member of the fly family of insects. Some mosquitoes are dangerous because they can spread diseases. The male mosquito is harmless. But the female mosquito feeds on the blood of animals or human beings. Her mouthparts have a piercing tube that sinks down through the skin into a blood vessel, enabling her to suck up blood. Sometimes she feeds on a diseased animal. When she next attacks an animal or a human being, she may pass on the disease. In tropical areas, certain kinds of mosquitoes spread malaria and yellow fever in this way.

Mosquitoes hatch from eggs laid on the surface of still water. The larvae hang just below the surface, breathing through two tiny air tubes at the end of their bodies. After one to five weeks, the larvae change into large comma-shaped pupae. About three days later, the pupae change into adult mosquitoes.

Mosquitoes can be controlled by spraying oil on the water in which they breed to prevent the larvae breathing; by putting special fish into the water to eat the larvae; or by spraying the adults with insecticides.

the spores are ripe, and a ring (or two rings) of tiny teeth attached to the rim and pointing inwards. The teeth open or close according to the amount of moisture in the air. In dry air, the teeth are open and the spores are shaken out by the wind.

A moss spore germinates into a highly branched, green, threadlike body called a *protonema*. The protonema gives rise to several new moss plants in a small clump.

When the moss plants are mature, the tips of the stems and branches develop

Red Square, in the center of Moscow beside the wall of the Kremlin, is nearly a quarter of a mile long. It is the scene of many military parades.

Mosses are leafy plants that grow in moist, shady places. Together with liverworts, mosses make up a division of simple plants that botanists call *Bryophta*. There are roughly 15,000 kinds of mosses in the world. They have no economic value, but are of interest to biologists because the first land plants were probably of this type. In addition, mosses are valuable as soil builders, since they are among the first plants to colonize new land.

Mosses reproduce by means of *spores*. The spores are carried in a capsule borne on a long stalk which arises from the crown of a moss stem. The capsule commonly has a little lid, which falls off when

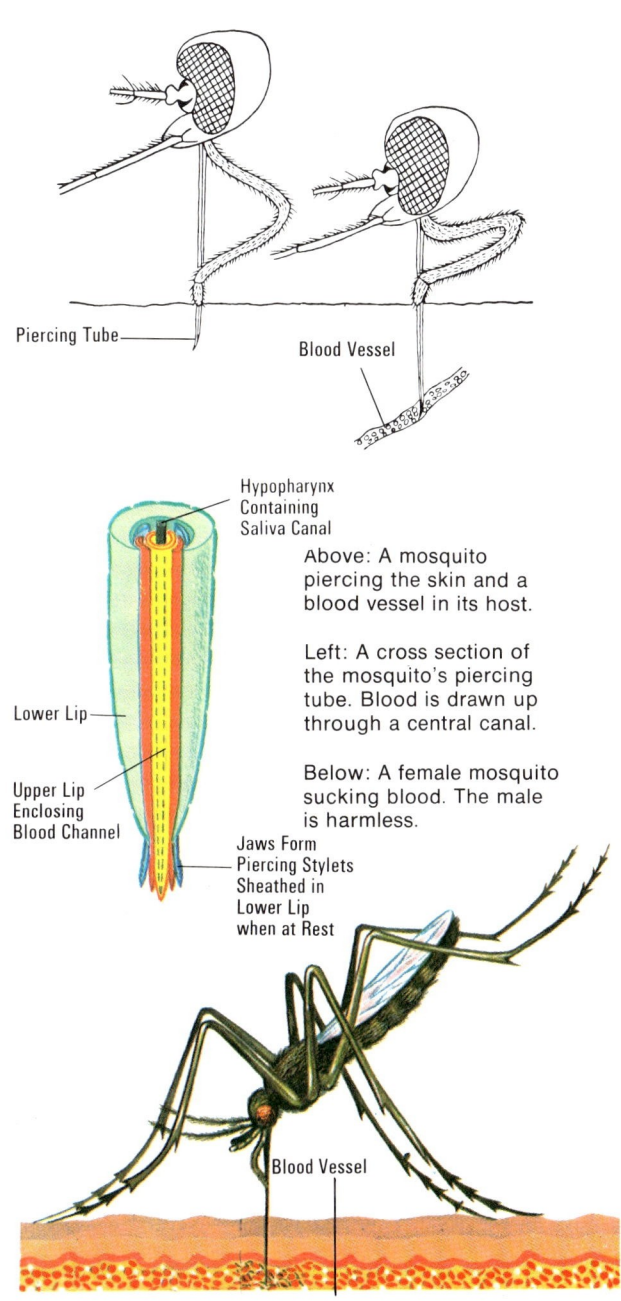

Above: A mosquito piercing the skin and a blood vessel in its host.

Left: A cross section of the mosquito's piercing tube. Blood is drawn up through a central canal.

Below: A female mosquito sucking blood. The male is harmless.

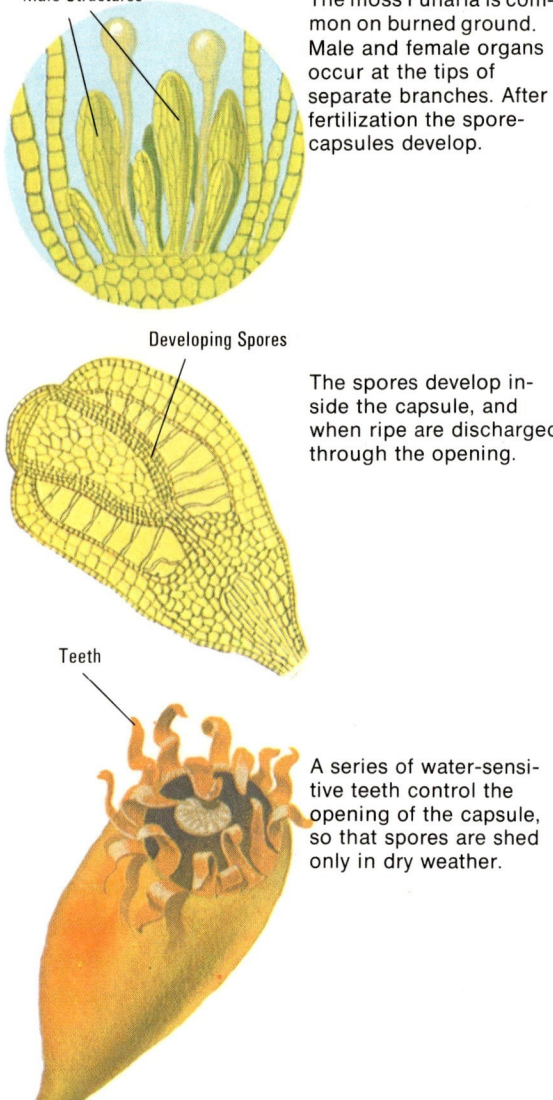

Male Structures — The moss Funaria is common on burned ground. Male and female organs occur at the tips of separate branches. After fertilization the spore-capsules develop.

Developing Spores — The spores develop inside the capsule, and when ripe are discharged through the opening.

Teeth — A series of water-sensitive teeth control the opening of the capsule, so that spores are shed only in dry weather.

sex organs. In wet weather the male cells are released, and swim to the female cells and fertilize them. The fertilized female cell develops a long stalk bearing a spore capsule at its top.

Mother Goose is a legendary figure who supposedly first told many of the children's stories that are well known today.

In 1697, a collection of well-known fables was published in France under the title *Tales of Mother Goose*. The book included the stories of *Sleeping Beauty*, *Cinderella* and *Puss in Boots*.

Later, the name Mother Goose came to be associated with collections of nursery rhymes such as "Humpty Dumpty", "Little Jack Horner" and "Old King Cole". No one knows the original authors.

Moths See Butterflies and Moths.

Motion pictures Going to the movies is one of the most popular forms of entertainment. We go to be thrilled by gun-battles and saloon brawls in westerns, delighted by the singing and dancing in colorful musicals, amused by animated cartoons, and informed by documentaries and newsreels. These are among the most important kinds of motion pictures.

The producer controls the making of commercial motion pictures. He supervises the whole project and helps to select the cast of actors and actresses to play in it. The director controls the actual filming of the scenes and is usually held to be responsible for the artistic quality of the final motion picture. The screen writer prepares the script from which the actors learn their lines. There are also many designers, craftsmen and technicians, including the film editors, or cutters, who have a vital role in shaping the final version of the movie.

The greater part of most movies is taken, or *shot*, in a motion picture studio. Realistic *sets*, or backgrounds, are built to resemble rooms, buildings and streets. Most of the sets are merely supported shells. Often scenes are taken on *location* outside the studio to heighten the realism. At the end of the filming, the exposed film strip in the cameras is processed. The director and film editors then choose the scenes to include in the motion picture and decide the order in which the shots will appear.

The cine camera works on the same principle as the still camera, but takes a series of still shots in quick succession. The film strip used is exactly the same as that used in still cameras. And it is *developed*, or processed in much the same way. (See Photography.)

The camera takes 24 separate shots,

The first public showings of motion pictures were given in France in 1895 by the Lumière brothers. Above: This movie of a train arriving at a station made people jump up to get out of the way. Above right: Movies were silent until 1927 and actors used exaggerated gestures and expressions to convey meaning. This scene is from *Way Down East* starring Mary Pickford. Right: Epic movies have been popular since World War I, and ancient Rome has probably been the subject of more epic movies than anything else. Below: a movie projector contains two sources of light, one to produce the picture and one to produce the sound.

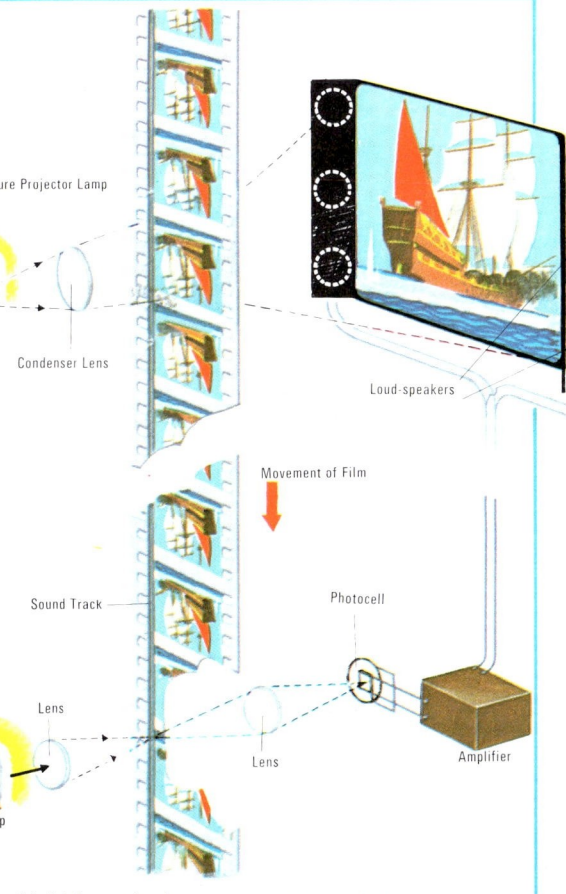

Light from the lamp passes through the sound track to the photocell, where a varying electric signal is produced as the film moves. The signal is amplified and fed to the loud-speakers.

Below: The scene in the studio filming *Captain Nemo and the Floating City*. The camera moves in for a close-up shot, and the microphone boom is kept out of the picture above the actors' heads.

or *frames*, every second. A claw mechanism holds the film strip still while each frame is shot and then moves the next frame into position. A half disc shields the film while it is being moved to prevent blurring of the image.

The sound for the movie is picked up by microphones suspended on long poles, or *booms,* above the actors but out of sight of the cameras. The microphone changes sound into a varying electric current. This current is converted into a varying pattern of light, which is recorded as a *sound track* on the edge of the film strip.

When the movie is completed, it can be shown through a *projector*. In the projector, a bright light from an electric-arc lamp shines through the film strip and throws a magnified image onto a

Scenes from the historical movie *Anne of a Thousand Days* (above) and the space age movie *Marooned* (below) show the wide range of subjects used by movie makers.

white screen. It projects 24 frames every second—the same rate at which the camera took them. It has a device for blocking off the light while the film is actually moving from frame to frame.

This means, of course, that the screen is dark between frames. But we do not notice this because our eyes continue to see the previous frame. This is called persistence of vision. It enables us to see the separate frames as a continuous moving picture.

Light-sensitive cells in the projector convert the sound track back into sound, which is relayed to loud-speakers behind the screen.

Early films, however, were silent. The first ones were made in 1895. But before then various people had invented devices which relied on the persistence of vision to give the illusion of movement. They included the *phenakistoscope* (1832), the *zoetrope* (1860), and the *kinetograph* (1868). In 1894, the American inventor Thomas Edison showed short films in a cabinet called a *kinetoscope*.

In 1895, movies were first projected successfully, and the motion picture industry had begun. Movies were first shown in fairgrounds and as items in vaudeville shows. However, theaters were soon built especially to show movies. Movies were sometimes called 'flicks' because of the flickering of the screen. This happened because they were projected at only 16 frames a second.

Until 1927, movies were silent. Pianists in the motion picture theaters provided background music to suit the action on the screen. However, most of the techniques of movie making were established in the days of silent motion pictures. One of the greatest of the early pioneers was David Wark Griffith (1880-1948). He was the first director to develop the 'close-up', the 'fade-out' and the 'flash-back' for dramatic effect. Griffith's *Birth of a Nation* (1915) was the first full-length motion picture.

In 1927, Al Jolson starred in *The Jazz Singer*, the first successful sound movie. From then on, the motion picture industry developed rapidly. In the 1950's, the wide-screen processes of Cinerama, Cinemascope and Todd-AO were introduced. The popularity of television caused a drop in attendance at movies in the 1950's and 1960's. However, movies of quality still attract audiences all over the world.

Motor cycle Gottlieb Daimler built not only one of the first automobiles but also the first motor cycle, in 1885. He fitted one of his gasoline engines to a bicycle frame. But today's motor cycles are highly specialized machines.

The engine of a motor cycle is similar in many respects to that of an automobile, but much smaller. It, too, has either a two-stroke or a four-stroke engine with gasoline as fuel. (See Automobile.) It may have one, two, three, or four cylinders, which are cooled by air or water.

The engine is started by kicking down a *kick-starter*. This turns the engine over and starts it firing, just like the self-starter on an automobile. The speed of the engine is controlled from a *twist-grip* on the handle-bars.

The gearbox is operated by a foot lever, and power is transmitted to the rear wheels by a chain drive. The clutch is operated by a hand lever on the handle-bars. So is the front brake. A foot pedal operates the rear brake.

Motor cycle racing at Monza, in Italy. There are important races in a large number of countries.

Mountains cover vast areas of the Earth's surface. The Rockies of North America, the Andes of South America, the Alps in southern Europe, and the Himalayas in Asia are among the largest and most spectacular of the world's mountain ranges. The Himalayas are the most magnificent of all. There lie many of the world's highest peaks including Everest (over 29,000 feet). Because of its height, the Himalaya range is often referred to as 'the roof of the world'.

Mountainous regions are often breathtakingly beautiful, with snowcapped peaks, ice-blue lakes, and cascading waterfalls. But they can also be extremely dangerous. Rock falls, avalanches, and treacherous weather conditions can turn even a simple mountain walk into a desperate fight for survival.

An example of North America's fine mountain scenery is this view of Mount Hood, an inactive volcano in the Cascade Range, North Oregon.

Mountains are a feature not only of the land, but also of the oceans. Sometimes these *submarine* mountains reach the surface of the ocean and form islands. The Bermuda Islands and the Azores are examples of this. The ocean bed, like the land, is criss-crossed with mountain ranges, plains, and deep valleys.

Mountains are formed as a result of movements in the Earth's crust. The devastating earthquakes that often occur in Persia, South America, Japan, and other regions provide us with a constant reminder of the fantastically powerful forces at work inside the Earth.

These earth movements give rise to three basic kinds of mountains—fold, block, and volcanic. *Fold mountains* form when two ancient land masses move towards each other and compress the land in between. The compression forces the land into great, wave-length folds. The Swiss Alps in Europe are examples of fairly

Mountain Building

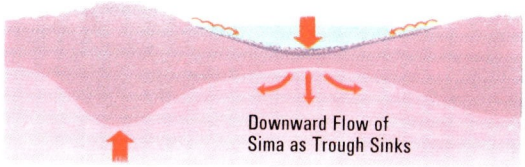

The first stage of the mountain building cycle. Sediments accumulate in the sinking trough.

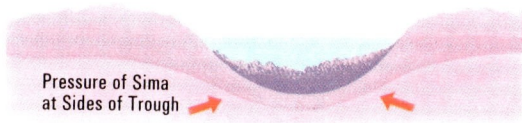

The trough fills at the expense of the rising land surrounding it.

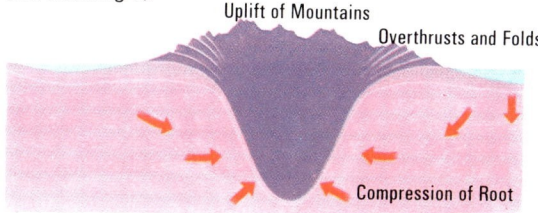

Stage three. The trough has been compressed, so that at the end of the second stage the sediments are buckled up and folded over the edges of the trough. The mountains gradually rise to regain balance.

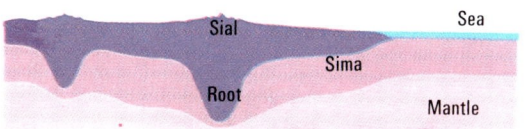

Mountain ranges and lowland plains behave in the same way as large and small icebergs, and tend to 'float' on the denser material below.

The most recent mountain system to be built stretches from western Europe to the Java Sea in Asia. It includes the European Alps (below).

young folds (about 15 million years old). The highlands of Britain are examples of old folds (about 240 million years old).

Sometimes earth movements may produce lines of weakness in the Earth's crust called *faults*. As the movements continue, great, block-like masses of the crust move along the line of the faults. They may subside below or be raised above the general land level to form *block mountains*, such as the Sierra Nevada in the United States. Long, deep valleys formed by land subsiding between parallel faults are called *rift valleys*. The best-known example of a rift valley is in East Africa and includes the Red Sea.

Volcanic mountains are heaps of volcanic ash and lava. Their growth is often very fast. In 1943, a Mexican farmer found a small hole in his field. Smoke coming out of the hole brought ash which covered his crops. Soon a volcanic cone began to form and lava started to flow from the hole. In 1952, volcanic activity ceased and the volcano, called Parícutin, stood 1,345 feet high.

From the day they are formed, mountains are subjected to the continuous action of the weather. The rain beats down, the sun scorches, and the frost freezes and shatters. Even the hardest rock becomes worn away in time. Rivers flow through and deepen the valleys. At high altitudes frozen 'rivers' of ice called *glaciers* form. They grind their way downwards widening and scarring the valleys.

Mouse A mouse is a small furry member of the order of gnawing mammals called *rodents* (see Rodents). Like its close relative the rat, the house-mouse is a pest that has followed man to almost every part of the world (see Rat). It does much damage in food stores, sleeping in quiet places during the day but coming out to feed at night. Mice breed rapidly, producing several litters each year. Man has used cats to catch mice for thousands of

Above: Mozart played the harpsichord at the age of three. At six he was taken on concert tours throughout Europe. The painting by Gustav Boulange shows Mozart playing in Vienna, Austria.

Left: A portrait of Mozart in his twenties.

years. But mice also make good pets. Some other kinds of mice are outdoor creatures. They include the harvest-mouse, which makes a globe-shaped nest among the stems of a wheat field.

Mozart, Wolfgang Amadeus (1756-1791), was one of the most outstanding composers of all time. He showed an astonishing ear for music when he was only three years old, and within a few years was able to play several instruments.

He was born in Salzburg, Austria, where his father was a musician at the court of the Archbishop of Salzburg.

Mozart began his professional career when he was six by touring Europe with his father and his sister, who was also extremely talented. They were acclaimed wherever they performed, and the young Mozart began to compose the first of his many works.

His great genius was his ability to compose virtually every form of music, including operas, choral music, orchestral music, and chamber music.

Mozart wrote some of the finest operas ever written, *The Marriage of Figaro, Don Giovanni,* and *The Magic Flute,* being particularly successful and popular. Among the forty symphonies that he composed, the *Jupiter* or *Symphony in C major,* the *Symphony in G minor,* and the *Symphony in E flat major* are regarded by many as his finest. Other notable works are the *Eine Kleine Nachtmusik,* which is a serenade, and the *Sinfonia Concertante,* a concerto for violin and viola.

Despite his successes he spent much of his life in poverty, and his health suffered as a result. He died when only thirty-five, and was buried in a pauper's grave in Vienna.

After his death, Mozart's works, which consisted of more than six hundred pieces, were classified by an Austrian scientist Ludwig von Köchel. Each composition is now to be found with the letter *K* and a number after it, for easy identification.

Muhammad (A.D. 570?-632) became one of the world's greatest religious leaders by founding the religion of Islam. His followers are called *Muslims*. Today, they number about 460 million. They do not worship Muhammad, but believe that he was the last messenger of *Allah* (God) and that he completed the teachings of such prophets as Abraham, Moses and Jesus.

Muhammad began his teaching in Mecca, Arabia. This print, of the 1700's, shows Kaaba, the chief sanctuary of Islam, in the center of the great mosque.

Muhammad was born in the Arabian city of Mecca. While meditating in the nearby mountains, he had a vision in which the Angel Gabriel commanded him to teach the 'true' religion. After Gabriel appeared to him again, Muhammad began to preach in Mecca. Most Arabs of his time worshiped many gods. But Muhammad told them of one God who required *Islam* (complete obedience).

The Meccans began to hate Muhammad for his criticisms of them. In A.D. 622, he fled to the neighboring city of Medina. Muslims begin their calender with the year of his flight, called the *Hegira*. Muhammad won many followers in Medina and became ruler of the city. Eight years later, he returned triumphantly to Mecca.

The people of Arabia were united under Islam. By A.D. 750, Muslims had carried Islam into other parts of the Middle East, North Africa and Asia. (See Islam.)

Muhammad, Elijah See Black Muslims.

Mummy A mummy is a specially preserved dead body. The name comes from an Arabic word 'mumiya', which means 'bitumen'; and this comes from a Persian word 'mum', which means 'wax'. Belief in a life after death has led many peoples to try to keep the bodies of their dead from rotting, so that the body would be ready for the return of the spirit. Preserved bodies have been found in caves in South America. It was the ancient Egyptians,

Slender minarets, or prayer towers, like this one in Tripoli, Libya, may be seen in all Muslim lands. They are usually attached to *mosques* (Muslim houses of worship), but some stand by themselves. From the top, a *muezzin*, or crier, calls the people to worship.

however, who really became masters of the art of *embalming* (preserving dead bodies). Bodies were drained of fluids, treated with preservatives, covered with bitumen, and then wrapped in linen cloths. This was the mummy; it was placed in a casket on which the dead person's face was painted.

Embalming the dead is not uncommon, today, in the United States. In the U.S.S.R. the dead leader Lenin has been embalmed. Lenin's body is on show in the Red Square in Moscow, though he died in 1924, but he is not wrapped up like a mummy.

Muscle is the fleshy tissue that controls the movement of our bodies. When we turn our heads, bend our arms, or pick up something, we use muscles.

These actions are all carried out by *voluntary* muscles — those under the conscious control of the brain. These are also called *skeletal* muscles, because they are attached to the skeleton, generally forming a bridge over a joint. The attachments are tough cords called *tendons*. When you want to move your arm, your brain sends a nerve signal to the arm muscles. These contract (shorten) and pull on the tendons which pull on

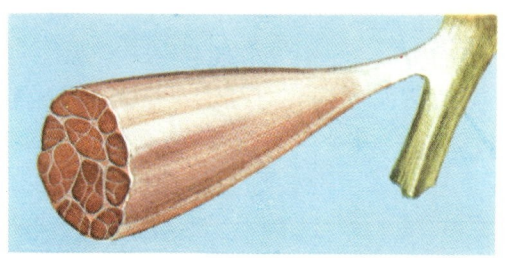

A muscle may be made up of many large bundles of muscle fibers. Each bundle is composed of smaller bundles of fibers.

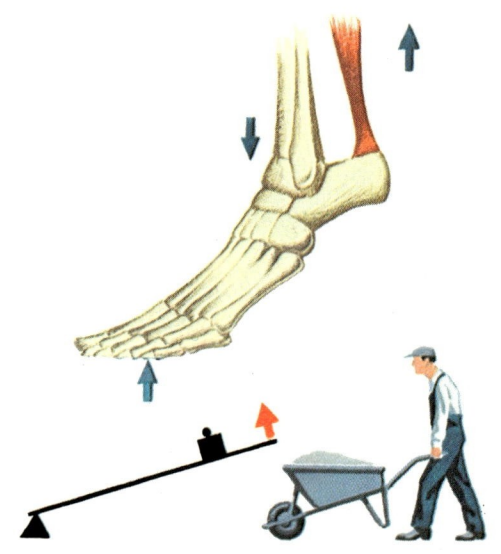

The Achilles tendon joins the calf muscle to the bone of the heel. In movement, the bone acts as a lever operated by the muscle, just as levers are used to move heavy weights.

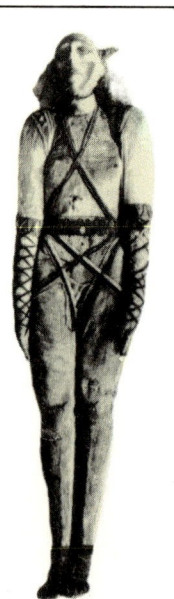

An Egyptian mummy. The body was soaked in chemicals, stuffed with sawdust, and wrapped in linen bandages. The mummy might be contained in the innermost of a series of coffins. The outer coffin is known as a Sarcophagus.

the arm bones to which they are attached, and the arm moves.

Some muscles are *involuntary* (not under conscious control). They do such jobs as opening and closing the ducts of glands, churning food in the stomach and regulating the size of blood vessels.

All muscles are composed of hundreds of fibers. Those of voluntary muscle are each about 1/250 of an inch thick and up to three inches long. They are marked with alternate light and dark bands. For this reason, voluntary muscle is also called *striped* muscle. The fibers of involuntary muscle have no markings, and so it is called *smooth* muscle. The fibers are also much smaller — only about 1/120 of an inch long and 1/4000 of an inch thick. The muscle of the heart—*cardiac muscle*—looks like striped muscle but functions like smooth muscle.

Museums are places where all kinds of objects of interest to people are stored and put on display. Such objects vary from coins and pottery to aircraft and skeletons of dinosaurs. Some things seen in museums may be of very little value while other objects may be almost priceless.

The first museums we know of were in Greece and Egypt during the third century B.C. The most famous of these was at Alexandria in the palace of the Ptolemy rulers of Egypt. Museums were unknown in the centuries which followed. During the fifteenth and sixteenth centuries rich men and scholars began to collect paintings and Greek and Roman objects, and in the seventeenth century objects of interest to scientists were also collected. These collections were often displayed in private museums. It was not until the nineteenth century that the idea of opening museums for everybody to use became common.

There are many kinds of museums today. Most countries have famous museums in which are kept objects collected from many lands. Among such museums are the British Museum (London), the Prado (Madrid), the Hermitage (Leningrad) and the Metropolitan (New York). Many large cities have good museums with general collections. There are also museums which display objects collected from the neighborhood or of interest to the local people. Some museums only keep objects connected with one subject, such as natural history, or science, or warfare; others display exhibits concerning the life of a famous person.

Most museums take great care to display objects well. Small articles are put in glass cases while big exhibits are hung on walls or put in large halls. Everything is arranged in subjects, and most articles

Above: Museums sometimes contain reconstructions of scenes from the past. This one, in the Smithsonian Institution, Washington, D.C. shows life among the now extinct Yosemite Indians of California.

Left: Formerly one of the old royal palaces of Paris, the Louvre was extended by Napoleon to house works of art plundered from foreign art galleries.

have labels giving information about them. The people who work in museums are experts who often write books about the most important things in their care. Sometimes old objects have to be carefully repaired or old paintings cleaned and restored, and this needs great skill.

In these and many other ways museums are interesting places which play an important part in storing and spreading knowledge. They also give pleasure to many people.

Mushrooms and toadstools look like little umbrellas growing in the ground. You find them in woods and fields, particularly in the autumn. Mushrooms and toadstools are among the commonest and certainly the most obvious members of a much larger group of plants called *fungi*. In common with all other fungi they have no chlorophyll and, as a result, are unable to make their own food (see Photosynthesis). Most live as *saprophytes* — that is, they extract their food from dead organic matter such as wood or soil humus. Some species, however, are *parasites* and get their food from living organisms.

The familiar umbrella you see is only a small part of the whole fungus. Most of it lies beneath the ground or buried deep in wood and consists of a mass of thin threads. The umbrella is merely the structure that bears the spores and is often called the *fruiting body* of the fungus. Spores are the means by which the mushroom or toadstool reproduces itself. It is important that the spores do not germinate near the parent plant, or many will perish. For this reason, the fruiting body appears above the ground so that wind currents will bear the spores far away.

The fruiting body bears the spores on a special layer of cells called a *hymenium*. There are several families, based upon the arrangement of the hymenium. In the *Agaricaceae*, to which typical mushrooms and toadstools belong, the hymenium is distributed over a number of plates called *gills*. The gills hang down from the underside of the umbrella, and fan out from the center like the spokes of a bicycle wheel. The corrugation caused by the gills greatly increases the surface of the hymenium and means that it can house far more spores than it could if it were flat. The top of the umbrella keeps the rain off the spores, while the stalk holds the hymenium well up to catch the wind. Some toadstools have *pores* on the underside of the cap rather than gills.

The fruiting body develops as a little ball beneath the ground. It then absorbs water and bursts out of the soil. The hymenium is commonly covered by a skin-like veil, which stretches from the rim of the cap to the top of the stalk. When the cap expands, the veil splits, leaving a little ring around the stalk. You can see this on a mushroom. The fruiting bodies of some species are completely enclosed in a membrane before they burst above the ground. The ruptured jacket then remains as a cup around the bottom of the stalk. A very poisonous toadstool called the *death cap* has both a ring around the top of the stalk and a cup at the bottom. Although many people pick and eat wild mushrooms there are many poisonous species, and only an expert should collect wild mushrooms for eating.

Opposite: The common mushroom starts life as a single thread, which branches and eventually joins another (top of page).

1. Horse Mushroom (*Agaricus arvensis*)
2. Oyster Mushroom (*Pleurotus ostreatus*)
3. Parasol Mushroom (*Lepiota procera*)
4. St. George's Mushroom (*Tricholoma gambosum*)
5. Turban fungus (*Gyromitra esculenta*)
6. Chanterelle (*Cantharellus cibarius*)
7. *Amanita caesarea*
8. Morel (*Morchella vulgaris*)
9. *Clitocybe geotropa*
10. *Boletus luridus*
11. Grisette (*Amanita vaginata*)
12. *Lactarius zonarius*
13. Shaggy Cap (*Coprinus comatus*)
14. *Lactarius volemus*
15. Cage fungus (*Clathrus cancellatus*)
16. *Clavaria flavia*

Bottom of page: When the fruiting bodies of the mushroom are nearly complete, they grow rapidly by absorbing water. The cap then breaks away from the stalk, exposing the gills.

Music is sound that people like to hear. It is made up of three elements: *melody, harmony* and *rhythm.*

A melody is a tune. Nearly all pieces of music contain tunes. Some are very easy to follow, such as the tune of a folk-song, or the latest recording of a 'pop' group. Others, such as the many little bits of tune in a *symphony* (a composition for orchestra), may be harder.

Harmony is what we call the combined sound when several notes are played at once. A group of such notes is called a *chord.* Sometimes musicians produce a form of harmony by playing two or more tunes at once, called *counterpoint.*

Rhythm is the regular 'beat' of music. It is the simplest kind of music known. The earliest men and, today, even very young children enjoy beating rhythms out on drums or even on pieces of wood. Rhythm is natural to man. He breathes regularly, his heart beats regularly and when he walks he puts his feet down rhythmically. The earliest musicians soon found that they could make different kinds of sounds to add to the rhythm. For example, they could sing or whistle notes of different *pitch*—that is, high or low—and could hit stones or blow through reeds to make different sounds, too.

The people of the early civilizations, such as those of Egypt and Greece, made music. But we do not know what it sounded like, because there was no way of writing it down or recording it.

Until the late Middle Ages, most music was played or sung for a specific purpose—for example, for dancing or working or as part of a religious service. Much old music that survives is church music.

By 1500, people were playing and singing music that was recognizably similar to the music of today. They had invented many instruments similar to violins and guitars, and trumpets, flutes and similar wind instruments.

A big advance in music came around 1600 with the invention of *opera,* a kind of play in which all the words are sung (see

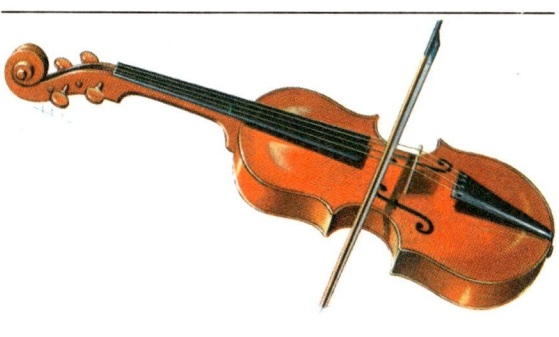

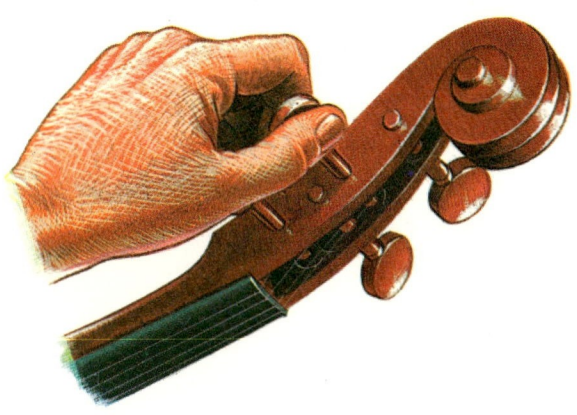

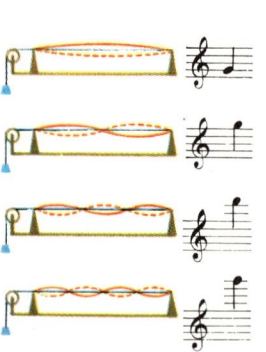

Above right: A string of given length and tension vibrates in several ways at the same time. The different vibrations produce harmonics. Top to bottom: Whole length of string produces fundamental note. One half of string produces 2nd harmonic. One third of string produces 3rd harmonic. One quarter of string produces 4th harmonic.

Above left: The body of the violin resonates when the strings are bowed.

Below left: The strings of a violin are tuned by being tightened or slackened. The player turns pegs to which they are attached while plucking or bowing the strings.

Below right: Countries all over the world have developed their own distinctive styles of music. The picture shows a flute player in Morocco.

Opera). An Italian, Claudio Monteverdi, was one of the earliest opera composers. He also formed one of the earliest *orchestras*, a large body of musicians. Counterpoint was the most popular way of writing music until the 1700's. Two Germans, J. S. Bach and G. F. Handel, were among the last and greatest writers of counterpoint. From the mid-1700's, musicians concentrated more on melody, with harmony to accompany it.

Orchestral music as we know it today was evolved and perfected by Joseph Haydn, Wolfgang Mozart, Ludwig van Beethoven and others in the late 1700's and early 1800's. Later musicians experimented with combinations of sounds and developed the possibilities of various instruments.

In the 1900's, musicians such as Arnold Schönberg have experimented with more difficult tunes and rhythms. Others such as Karl-Heinz Stockhausen have used tape recorders to produce new kinds of instruments and sounds.

Greek women playing harp, cithara, and lyre. (Fifth century B.C.)

Musical Instruments produce sound in many ways. But they all depend on vibrations to produce sound waves in the air.

In *stringed* instruments, a stretched string vibrates. The violin, viola, cello, and double bass each have four strings, which are caused to vibrate with a bow or by plucking. The player varies the pitch of each string by pressing it at one point against a finger-board—the shorter the length of the vibrating string, the higher the pitch of the sound. The heavier strings produce lower notes.

Stringed instruments such as the guitar, harp, lute and banjo are always plucked. The guitar, lute and banjo have *frets* on the finger-board to help the player place his fingers accurately. On the harp, there is a separate string for each note, although the length of each string can be varied by pressing pedals at the base.

In the dulcimer, which like the harp has separate strings for each note, the strings are struck by hammers. In the piano, the strings are struck by hammers operated by a keyboard (see Pianoforte). Other keyboard instruments with strings are the harpsichord, in which the strings are plucked by quills, and the clavichord, in which they are struck by metal wedges.

In *wind* instruments a column of air vibrates. In woodwind instruments, the vibration is caused by a *reed* attached to a mouthpiece, as in clarinets and saxophones; by a double reed, as in oboes and bassoons; or by blowing across a hole in the instrument, as in flutes and piccolos. All woodwind instruments have holes that are covered by the fingers or by pads operated by the fingers. These alter the length of the vibrating column of air—the shorter the column the higher the pitch. In the recorder, a whistle or fipple mouthpiece causes the vibration.

In *brass* instruments, the vibration is caused by the player's lips vibrating in a cup-shaped or cone-shaped mouthpiece. The air column vibrates from the mouthpiece to the *bell* of the instrument. Several notes can be blown in this way, and these are the notes used in bugle calls. In brass instruments other than the bugle, the air column can be lengthened. In horns, trumpets, and tubas, the air column is diverted into pieces of side-tubing by pressing valves or pistons.

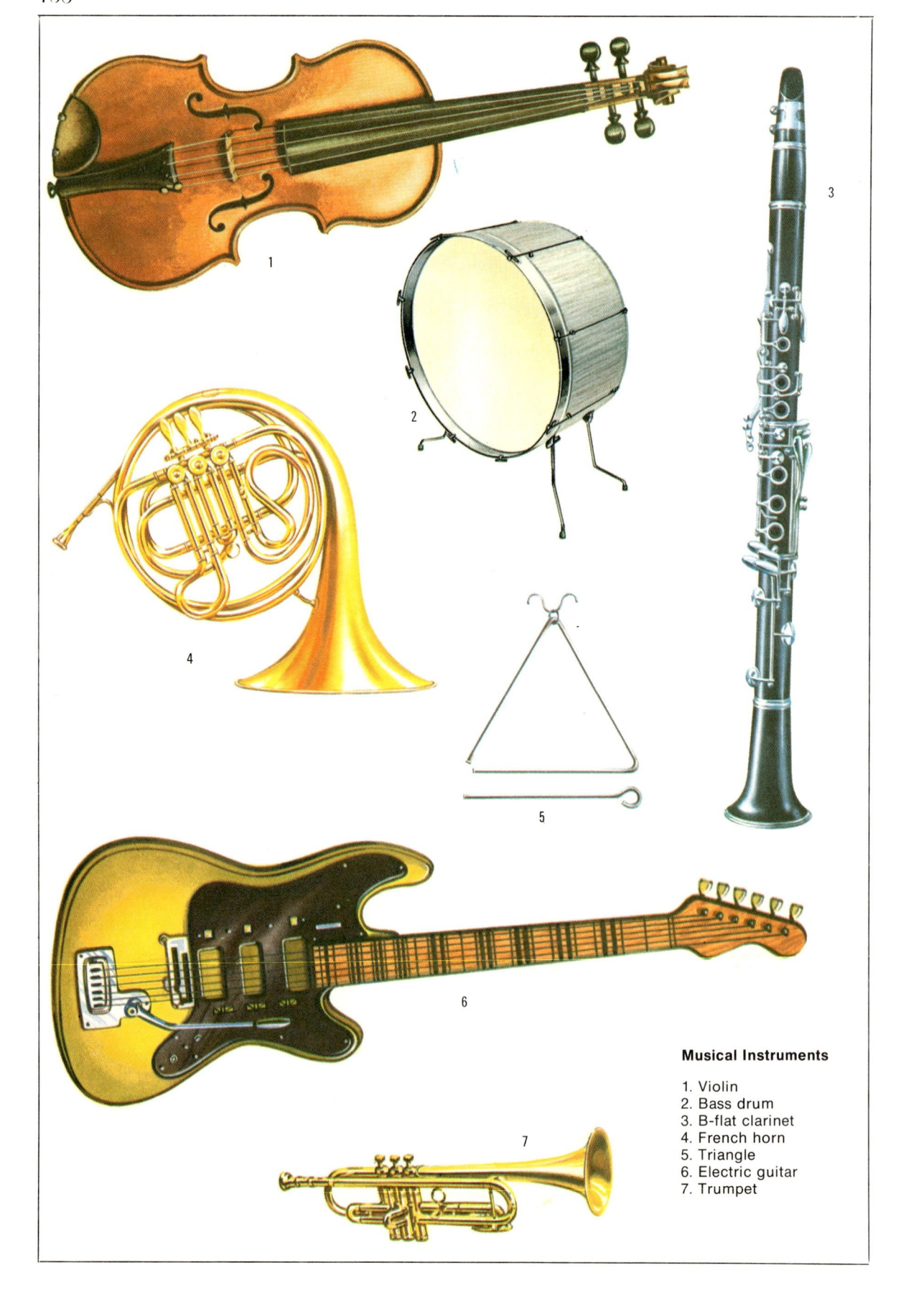

Musical Instruments

1. Violin
2. Bass drum
3. B-flat clarinet
4. French horn
5. Triangle
6. Electric guitar
7. Trumpet

Six more notes are obtained in this way for each note obtained by a certain lip pressure. In the trombone, the slide is moved to vary the length of the air column.

The organ is also a wind instrument of a kind. Each note is produced by a separate pipe into which air is blown by pressing a key (see Organ).

In *percussion* instruments, a taut skin or a piece of metal or wood is struck to produce a note. The note is usually of short duration. There are two kinds of percussion instruments: *definite pitch* or *tuned* percussion and *indefinite pitch* percussion. Tuned instruments include the timpani—large drums in which the tension of the skins can be varied. In the vibraphone and xylophone, metal or wooden bars tuned to various notes and arranged like the piano keyboard are struck with mallets. In the celeste, small hammers separated by a keyboard strike metal plates. Indefinite pitch instruments include drums, cymbals, gongs, tambourines, and triangles.

Several popular and folk-music instruments depend on the vibration of reeds to produce the sound, without causing an air column to vibrate as in woodwind instruments. The mouth-organ, concertina, and accordion have a reed for each note. The mouth-organ is blown directly, but the concertina and the accordion have bellows to produce the air flow. In bagpipes, a set of vibrating reeds produces the drone. The tune is played by a chanter with holes like a woodwind instrument. The bag is blown up by the mouth and squeezed under the arm to produce the air flow.

In many modern musical instruments, the sound is produced by electrical means, amplified, and fed to a loudspeaker. The most popular instruments of this kind are the electric guitar and the electronic organ.

Nails and claws are made up of hardened skin and a horny substance called *chitin*. In human beings, nails grow from the fingertips and toes, and are of little use, but animals use their claws for defense and attack. Sharp claws are often called *talons*, and birds of prey and wild cats may use their talons to slash and kill their prey, and to carry it off. Hoofs are similar to nails, except that they are blunt.

Names are given to many things to identify them. Most names have an original meaning quite different from the character of the person or object to which they are given. Many people are called *Smith*, but they do not shoe horses or work metal for a living, as a *smith* does.

Personal names usually consist of at least two names: a first name and a *surname*. In between, there may be more names, such as more first names and family names. First names are also called *Christian* names, because they may be conferred on a child at a christening or baptism. First names may be descriptive in meaning: *Benedict* and *Clement* come from Latin words meaning *blessed* and *merciful*, respectively; *Helen* comes from Greek and means *bright*; *Grace* means what it says. First names may also have religious origins, particularly Hebrew. *John* means *Jehovah is good*, and *Elizabeth* means *God is good fortune*. Family names are surnames used as first names.

Surnames may also be descriptive. *Black*, *Brown* and *White* are common examples, perhaps originally referring to the color of someone's hair. Many surnames are descriptive of an occupation, such as *Smith*, *Turner*, *Shepherd*, *Glover* and *Baker*. Some surnames derive from places, such as *Hill*, *Brooks* and *Ford*, and even cities, such as *London* or *Washington*. Many surnames have suffixes or prefixes meaning *son of*. *Fitz* or *Mac* at the start of a surname, and *son* at the end, all mean *son of*.

Place names are more accurate when descriptive. Many end in *ton*, *ham*, *burg*, *wick* or *worth*, all of which are various terms for groups of dwellings.

Napoleon Bonaparte (1769-1821) was one of the greatest soldiers in the history of warfare. After the French Revolution of 1789 had overthrown King Louis XVI and set up a republic, there were many great opportunities for ambitious men who could restore order. Napoleon Bonaparte rose to power rapidly—he was a military genius with a brilliant command of strategy. He was given power to bring order back into the country, but his ambitions for France led him to create an empire.

Napoleon was born at Ajaccio, on the island of Corsica, which belongs to France. He went to a cadet school at Brienne and to the leading military school in Paris. By 1792 he was a captain of artillery, and three years later saved the republic by crushing a royalist rebellion in Paris. With 30,000 starving, ragged soldiers, he took control of Lombardy, a province of Italy, and later won Belgium and some territory from Austria. In 1799 he saved the republic from rioters again. He seized power and ruled as a dictator. In 1804 he crowned himself emperor in the presence of Pope Pius VII in Paris.

In spite of many victories in Europe, Napoleon was hampered by Britain's superior sea power. Nelson's defeat of the French and Spanish at Trafalgar in 1805 crushed Napoleon's hopes of invading England. Napoleon won further victories against the Austrians and the Prussians, and made his brothers Joseph and Louis kings of Naples and Holland. But his attempt to stop all European countries from trading with England failed entirely when Russia would not co-operate. He took a great army to Russia in the winter of 1812 to force Tsar Alex-

Above: A portrait of Napoleon at the age of thirty-six, by Robert Lefèvre.

Left: The zenith of Napoleon's career. In 1804 he crowned himself Emperor of the French in Notre Dame, and received the Pope's blessing. Napoleon's decision to become Emperor antagonized many prominent people who had previously considered him an influence for good. This painting of the coronation is by J. L. David.

ander to help, but the campaign ended in disaster.

Napoleon met his final defeat at Waterloo, by the combined forces of Britain under Wellington, and Prussia under Blucher, in June 1815. Napoleon surrendered to the British and was exiled on the island of St Helena, where he died in 1821.

Napoleon was a short man, and his stature earned him the nickname 'the little corporal'. He was adored by his soldiers, and fired by great ambition. His rise to power was helped by the influence of his first wife, the beautiful Josephine de Beauharnais.

Napoleonic Wars The French Revolution made France many enemies in Europe and resulted in a series of wars which lasted with hardly a break from 1792 until 1815. During these wars France found

Left: The French bivouac on the eve of the battle of Austerlitz. This was possibly the most conclusive of all Napoleon's battles. By brilliant tactics he crushed a combined Russian and Austrian army, and caused the break-up of the Holy Roman Empire.

Below left: The meeting of Napoleon and Francis II after Austerlitz; Francis was the Holy Roman Emperor, and had taken the title of Emperor of Austria. Napoleon created the Confederation of the Rhine in 1806. This deprived Francis of his German title, but was a major step in the creation of modern Germany.

Below: Early in Napoleon's career he had dreams of an Eastern empire. But his fleet was destroyed by Nelson at the Battle of the Nile. From that point onwards Napoleon was severely hampered by British naval supremacy.

a brilliant general in Napoleon Bonaparte. He won many victories, became sole ruler of France, and crowned himself emperor in 1804. But Napoleon's ambitions did not stop with the crown of France; he dreamed of ruling the rest of Europe as well. Consequently, the wars became a struggle against the ambitions of one man and for this reason are known as the Napoleonic Wars.

The chief enemies of France were Austria, Prussia, Russia, Britain and Spain. The French armies were large, well-led and well-trained. They won many battles, the most important being at Marengo and Hohenlinden (1800), at Austerlitz (1805) and at Jena (1806). These victories gave Napoleon control over most of Europe.

However, the British navy was very powerful and in Lord Nelson Britain had an outstanding admiral. Nelson destroyed a French fleet at the battle of the Nile (1798) and so dashed Napoleon's hopes of conquering the East. Seven years later, Nelson defeated the main French fleet at Trafalgar and ended Napoleon's plans to invade Britain.

Napoleon next tried to ruin Britain by stopping all her trade with Europe. But the people of Europe needed British products and grew restless when goods became scarce and expensive. In 1808 the Spanish rebelled against Napoleon. A small British army, commanded by Arthur Wellesley, later Duke of Wellington, was sent to help them. Wellington won a number of battles and this persuaded Russia to re-enter the conflict. Napoleon led a huge army into Russia in 1812, but most of his 600,000 soldiers were killed in battle or perished in the bitter conditions of the Russian winter.

Encouraged by this disaster, Britain,

The Battle of Waterloo, from a painting by Sir William Allan. Soon after his escape from Elba, Napoleon suffered his final and most crushing defeat at the hands of the Duke of Wellington and the Prussian Prince Blücher.

Europe in 1812
At this period Napoleon was virtually master of Europe, with the only effective opposition coming from Britain and Russia, who were eventually joined by Prussia, Austria and Sweden. 1812 was the year of Napoleon's fateful Russian Campaign, which heavily depleted his forces and marked the beginning of his downfall.

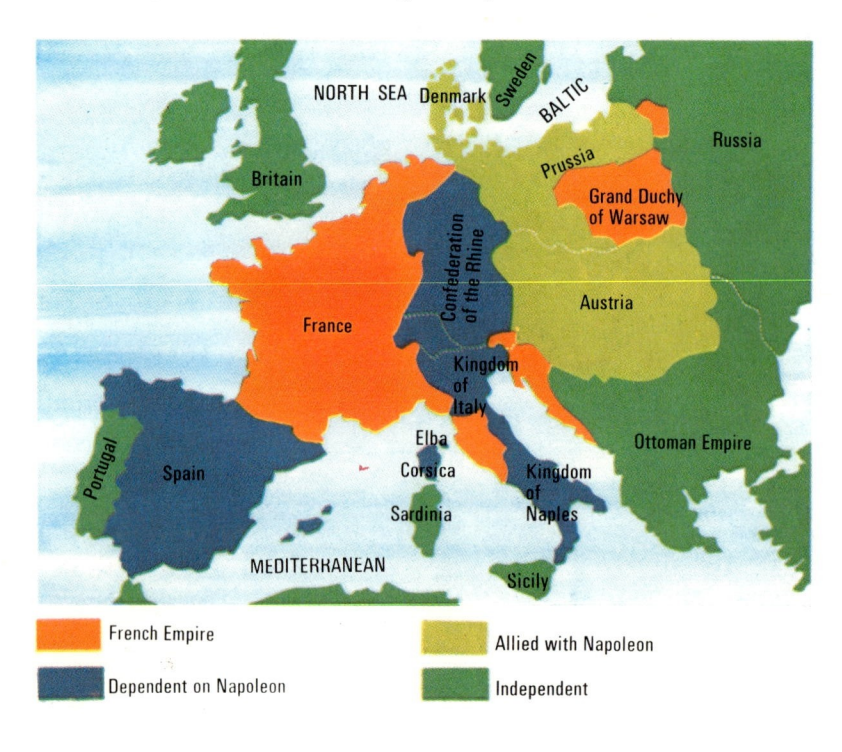

Prussia, Russia, Austria and Sweden united against Napoleon. Their armies drove deep into France and occupied Paris (1814). Napoleon was banished to the island of Elba. In 1815 he escaped and rallied the French armies but was finally defeated on the battlefield of Waterloo by British and Prussian forces.

Peace had come at last to Europe. Napoleon was exiled to St Helena, and the countries of Europe were handed back to their traditional rulers.

Nashville is the capital of Tennessee. It lies in the north of the state, on the Cumberland River. Nashville is a transportation, commercial and educational center. With a population of 444,000, it is the second largest city in Tennessee.

Nashville's largest single industry is publishing. The many manufactured products include man-made fibers, clothing, shoes, vehicle parts, farm machinery, glass and rubber.

Music has played an important part in the life of the city for many years. It is the home of the 'Grand Ole Opry' and the Country Music Hall of Fame, and is an important recording center.

In 1779, Fort Nashborough was built on the site of the present city. In 1784, Nashville was given its present name, and in 1843 it became the official capital of Tennessee. During the Civil War, the city was taken by Union troops who used it as a base. After the war, Nashville became an industrial center.

National Anthems are patriotic songs played and sung on ceremonial occasions. They are played during national festivities and as greetings to visiting sovereigns and heads of state. They are played also at many public gatherings, from serious political rallies to sporting events, according to the customs of the country. The singing may be done by a solo performer, or by everyone present. Sometimes, the anthem is merely played, and no one sings.

The words of a national anthem praise the nation and its people. Many of these songs are concerned with wars and revolutions. *The Star-Spangled Banner* was written during the War of 1812 by Francis Scott Key. In 1814, Key was being held prisoner on a British warship when he saw the shelling of Fort McHenry near Baltimore. After a day of bombardment, Key saw through the mist that the American flag was still flying. The sight inspired him to write most of the words of *The Star-Spangled Banner* in a few minutes. The anthem is sung to music by John Stafford Smith. Congress approved the song as the national anthem in 1931.

France's rousing national anthem, called *The Marseillaise*, was written to honor the citizen-soldiers of the city of Marseilles, who marched to the relief of Paris during the French Revolution. Translated into English, it begins 'Forward, children of our country. The day of glory has come.' It was written and composed by a French soldier, Rouget de l'Isle, in 1792. The composer of the British anthem, *God Save the Queen,* is unknown, but the song was first sung in 1745, shortly after the Jacobite rebellion against the Crown had been crushed.

The French National anthem was written by Rouget de l'Isle. This somewhat romantic painting shows him singing *The Marseillaise* in front of a group of friends.

Patriotic fervor runs high in defense of a nation. Thus Mexico's anthem begins: 'Mexicans, at the call of war, Seize your swords and bridles!'

Governments frequently borrow money from the International Monetary Fund. Members of this organization are shown here meeting in Istanbul, Turkey.

National Debt A country's national debt is the amount of money its government has borrowed from the people of the country and from other countries. Governments often borrow money when they need more money than they receive from taxes and other normal sources of revenue. Generally, the money they borrow is spent on such projects as building roads, hospitals, schools or hydroelectric installations. In times of war a country's national debt always increases because of the vast amount of extra money that the government has to spend. Governments raise loans by selling bonds, certificates, and loan stocks to private individuals and institutions. Among the institutions, banks and insurance companies are often the largest buyers of government bonds and loan stocks. Many people invest their savings in government bonds or certificates to earn interest.

The money that a government borrows from other countries or from international bodies such as the International Monetary Fund is called its *external national debt*. A large external national debt greatly strains a country's resources.

National parks These are special areas set aside in many countries to protect

A view of Carlsbad Caverns National Park in New Mexico. Among the attractions of these beautiful caves are limestone columns called stalactites and stalagmites.

wild-life, plant life and beautiful scenery. Governments pass laws to forbid hunting, building, mining, farming or forestry in national parks.

National parks became necessary because the growth of the world's population threatened animals and plants in many parts of the world. Vast forests were cut down and grasslands were plowed or used for grazing cattle and sheep. Farmers often killed wild animals because they damaged crops or attacked livestock. Other animals died because the plants they fed on were cut down or burned. Others, such as the bison that roamed the North American plains, nearly disappeared because men killed them in vast quantities for their skins and meat.

Men in some countries first saw the danger to wildlife and the wonders of nature hundreds of years ago. In 1542, an area was established in Switzerland where hunting was forbidden. The first American national park was established in 1872, at Yellowstone in the northwestern United States. Covering 3,471 square miles, Yellowstone is the largest national park in the United States. It contains several *geysers*—hot springs that *erupt* (force upwards) tall columns of steam and boiling water.

By the late 1960's, the United States

Right: Lions in Wankie Game Reserve, Rhodesia. Below: Bison in Banff National Park, Alberta, Canada. Many national parks are created in order to protect wild animals in their natural surroundings.

had 32 national parks. They are administered by the National Park Service, a bureau of the United States Department of the Interior. The bureau was set up in 1916 to take charge of the areas that had been made into national parks. The National Park Service has four regional headquarters: Richmond, Virginia; Omaha, Nebraska; Sante Fe, New Mexico; and San Francisco, California. Its duties include preventing forest fires and the pollution of streams, and safeguarding animal and plant life in the parks. Animals protected by the service include elk, caribou, deer, bears, mountain sheep and bison. National parks of outstanding scenic beauty include the Grand Canyon, in northwestern Arizona. The 673,203-acre park includes 105 miles of the remarkable gorge cut by the Colorado River. The Isle Royale National Park, which lies on the largest island in Lake Superior, is noted for its forests and herds of moose.

Africa has many great parks, including the 8,000 square-mile Kruger National Park in South Africa. There, visitors can see and photograph elephants, lions and many other animals roaming freely in their natural surroundings. Some Australian parks protect rare plants and such animals as the koala bear.

Today, most countries of the world have national parks. In many countries of Africa, tourists from all over the world arrive to see the magnificent wildlife.

Natural gas is a mixture of gases which is often found where there is petroleum. But it is also found on its own. Natural gas has become an important fuel. It may be used by itself, or mixed with coal gas or oil gas.

Like petroleum, natural gas is composed of compounds of hydrogen and carbon, called *hydrocarbons,* which have a high heat value. The main hydrocarbons are methane, ethane, propane and butane.

The United States and Russia are the world's biggest producers of natural gas. There are also vast gas fields in Canada, North Africa and the Middle East. In Europe, natural gas is produced from fields in Italy and France and under the North Sea.

Methods of prospecting and drilling for natural gas are similar to those used for petroleum. But great care is taken as the supply is struck because the gas is usually under great pressure and may also be very hot.

Pipelines, often hundreds of miles long,

Natural Gas

An off-shore drilling rig.

Right: Looking down the drill pipe. The helicopter is a valuable asset when the sea is rough.

Below: The drilling platform. This rig is in the North Sea, between Britain and the mainland of Europe.

Some Historical Navigating Instruments

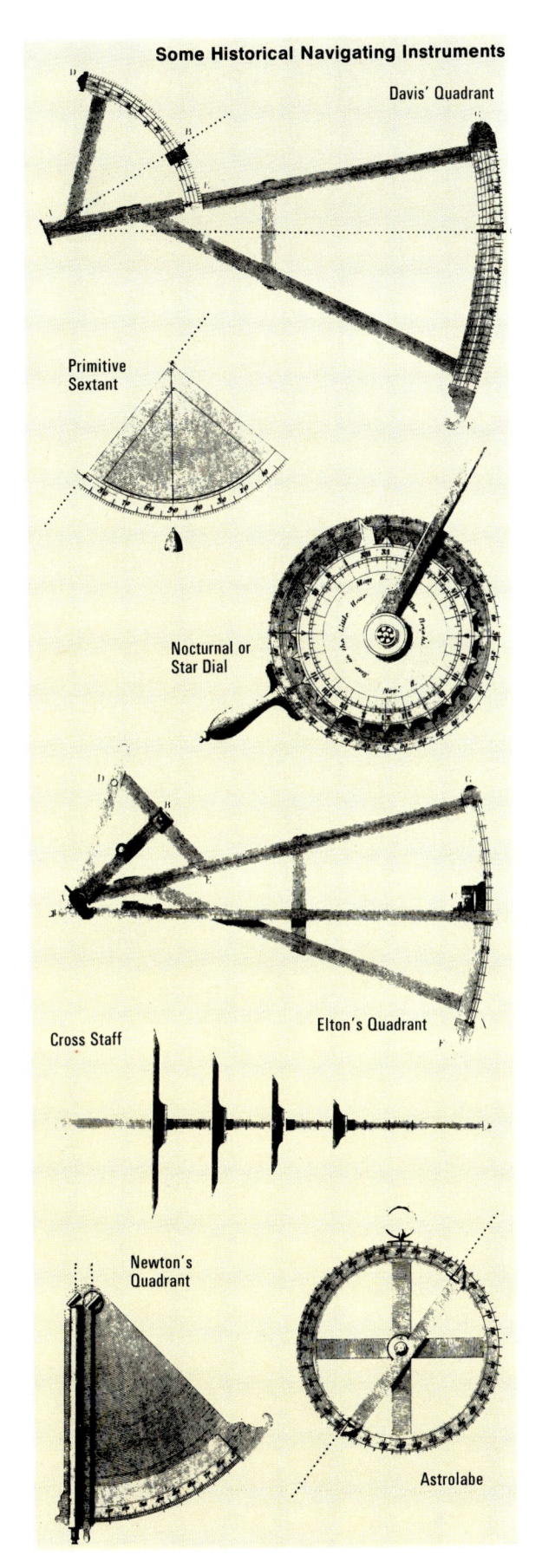

Davis' Quadrant

Primitive Sextant

Nocturnal or Star Dial

Cross Staff

Elton's Quadrant

Newton's Quadrant

Astrolabe

carry the gas to processing plants where it is purified. The gas may be piped directly as a fuel or it may be liquefied by cooling so that it can be transported to other countries.

A great deal of natural gas is used as a raw material for the chemical industry in much the same way as petroleum is. Plastics, dyes, explosives and drugs are some of the valuable end products.

Navigation is the method of finding one's way about the Earth's surface. Navigation is relatively easy on land. With the aid of good maps one can find one's way when walking in unknown country by observing landmarks. Road signs and other information help car drivers to navigate. But the navigator of a ship or an aircraft has no signs or landmarks to tell him where he is and in which direction he is going. Furthermore, ocean currents and winds may take the ship or aircraft off course. The navigator must check his position frequently and determine in which direction the ship or aircraft should be heading.

The navigator makes an estimate of his position by *dead reckoning*—he calculates the course of the ship from a known position by measuring its speed and time of travel, allowing for currents and winds. But to make sure that he is on course, he must make accurate measurements of his position on the Earth's surface. There are two main ways of doing this: *celestial navigation* and *radio navigation*.

Celestial navigation depends on observations of the stars, Sun, Moon, and planets. The navigator uses a sextant to measure the angle a heavenly body makes with the horizon. (See Sextant.) Observations of the Sun give him a rough position, but to find it accurately he must observe the stars. He measures the angle or altitude of a certain star in the sky, its *bearing* (direction), and notes the exact time of the observation. By consulting tables, he finds the point on the Earth's surface directly below the star at that time. This is called the *substellar point*. The altitude of the star tells him how far he is from the substellar point, and he draws a line on his chart this distance from the substellar point and at right-angles to its bearing. This line is called a *line of position,* and the ships is somewhere along the line. By making observations of two more stars, he draws two other lines of position on the chart, and they cross at one point. This is the ship's position.

Radio navigation depends on observations of radio signals sent out by stations on shore or by satellites. Several shore stations send out signals of rapid *synchronized* pulses—that is, pulses sent out at exactly the same time. As the shore stations are at different distances from the ship, the signals take slightly different times to reach the ship and will be slightly out of synchronization. This gives the distances of the shore stations from the ship. In addition, their bearings can be found by using a rotating loop aerial. If the positions of the shore stations are known, the position of the ship can be found either from their distances or their bearings. *Satellite* navigation systems have been established by the United States. A series of satellites orbit the Earth broadcasting their exact positions as special signals. A computer on board the ship receives the signals, measures the change in signal as the satellites passes overhead (the Doppler shift), and calculates the ship's position to within 200 yards. The operation is entirely automatic. The liner *Queen Elizabeth 2* is fitted with this navigation system.

Once the navigator knows the ship's true position, he must make sure that the ship is heading in the right direction. This is done by using a *compass*. Magnetic compasses always point to the Earth's magnetic poles. (See Magnetic poles.) A gyrocompass contains a flywheel spinning in a set direction. Once set to north, it does not move whatever the direction of the ship.

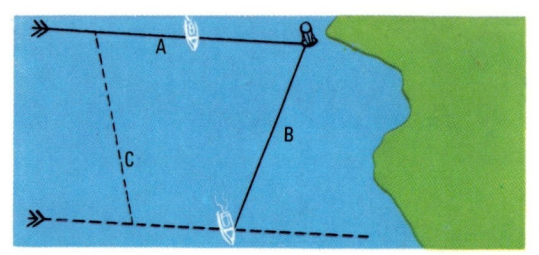

A diagram to illustrate the principle of a running fix. Line A is the first bearing, Line B represents the second bearing, taken half an hour later. Line C is the actual distance traveled during that time

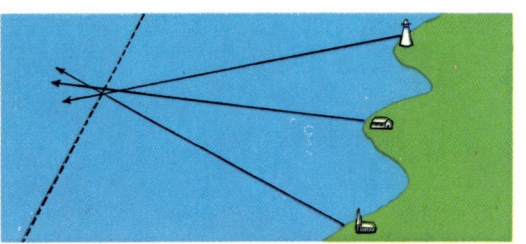

Three cross-bearings form a small triangle or 'cocked hat', because of unavoidable minor inaccuracies.

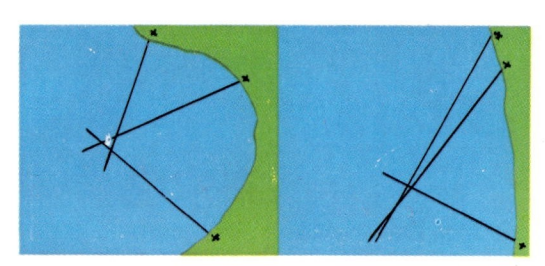

Left: If the triangle has roughly equal sides, it is safe to assume that the ship is in the center. Right: A bad cocked hat. The triangle has unequal sides and the bearings must therefore be checked.

When a ship leaves port, it is guided by a pilot who knows the harbor. Near the coast, the navigator works by taking bearings of landmarks on the coast. Accurate navigation is essential if the ship is to avoid dangerous rocks, and the navigator must know exactly where his ship is on a chart of the area. When he is out of sight of land, he depends on celestial or radio navigation methods. Aircraft depend mostly on radio navigation, because they move so fast the navigator or pilot needs results quickly. On landing, *radar* is used to make a continual check on the airplane's position. Ships use radar to find their way in fog. (See Radar.)

Nazism is the name by which Adolf Hitler's National Socialist ideas came to be known. Hitler helped build up the Nazi party after Germany's defeat in the First World War. His ideas were very extreme, and his followers were trained like soldiers.

Hitler came to power legally after the slump of 1929-32. During this crisis, six million Germans were unemployed, and many people voted for the Nazis hoping they could solve Germany's problems. Once in power, Hitler set up concentration camps for his opponents, abolished other political parties, and controlled all newspapers, radio and films. He insisted that as 'Aryans', Germans were a master race, destined to rule the world. Jews and Gypsies were systematically persecuted and murdered because they were considered members of inferior races. Unemployment was solved by expanding the armed forces and the armament industries. Then Hitler began seizing other countries, first Austria and part of Czechoslovakia in 1938. During World War II, with his ally Mussolini of Italy, Hitler's armies occupied most of Europe. He committed suicide in Berlin in 1945 when Germany was defeated.

Above: The Nazis were fond of staging huge open-air gymnastic displays to demonstrate their 'master race' concept.

Left: A flag display by the Hitler Youth.

Below: Tanks roll past the saluting post during Hitler's 49th birthday celebrations in Berlin.

Nebraska is a state in the Great Plains region of the midwestern United States. Covering an area of 77,227 square miles, it is bordered by the Missouri River in

The map shows the location of Nebraska.

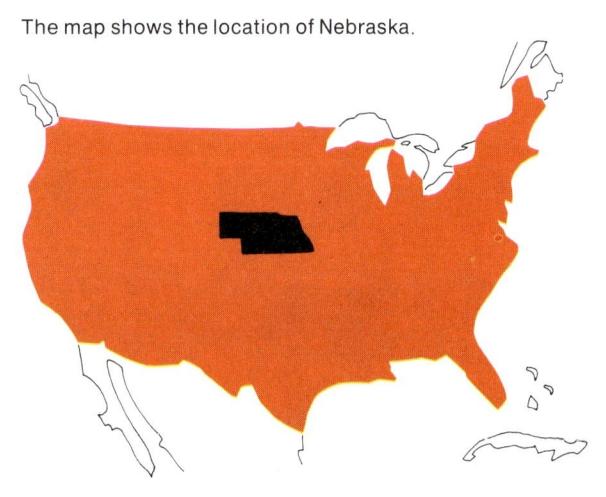

A mechanical harvester is used to gather a bumper wheat crop in Nebraska. Aided by mechanization, farmers produce large crops on Nebraska's fertile plains.

the northeast and by Colorado in the southwest. Elsewhere, it is bordered by Wyoming, South Dakota, Iowa, Missouri and Kansas.

Most of Nebraska's 1,408,000 people work as farmers on the fertile farmlands, especially in the east. Leading crops include corn, sugar beet, wheat and other grains. Omaha, Nebraska's largest city, Lincoln, the capital, and other major towns are in this region. Industries include production of farming machinery and chemicals as well as meat packing and food processing. In north-central Nebraska, huge herds of cattle graze. Much wheat grows in the plains of the west.

The United States bought the area of present-day Nebraska from France, as part of the Louisiana Purchase, in 1803. In 1867, Nebraska was admitted to the Union as America's 37th state.

Nebula is a name originally given to all kinds of misty objects in the sky whose real nature could not be discovered with the telescopes of the early astronomers. Some are distant galaxies. Others are star clusters and clouds of dust and gas within our own galaxy.

Some of the clusters are spherical in form, like a giant ball of stars, densely packed in the center but spaced farther apart at the outside. They are beautiful objects when seen in a telescope. They have been found inside other galaxies as well as our own.

The gaseous nebulae occur in two main forms—bright and dark. The bright ones are clouds of hot gas, mostly hydrogen. The best known example is in the constellation Orion, surrounding the middle star of the three said to represent Orion's sword. It can just be seen with the unaided eye on a clear night as a faint misty patch.

The dark nebulae are clouds of cool

The Orion nebula as seen through a high-power telescope. This bright nebula, surrounding the middle of the three stars said to represent Orion's sword, is a cloud of hot gas, mostly hydrogen. Stars are probably still being 'born' within the nebula.

dust and gas which obscure the light from the stars beyond.

Negro history Before about A.D. 1500, Negro history is largely the story of Africa. Anthropologists class the great majority of Africans south of the Sahara desert as Negroes. From the early 1500's to the mid-1800's, millions of Africans were taken as slaves to the Americas by European slave traders. After about 1510, therefore, Negro history concerns the Americas.

Perhaps as early as 2000 B.C., African peoples living in the grassland regions south of the Sahara formed settled farming villages. In the 1000's B.C., people living in the area of Nok (in what is now northern Nigeria) developed fine pottery, metalwork and *terracotta* (hardened clay) sculpture. Meanwhile, in northeastern Africa, the kingdom of Meroe developed into a powerful state. Its people, who had learned the art of iron working from ancient Assyria, traded and conquered wide-

Left: A young African girl, with traditional hairstyle and jewelry. Right: A group of American Negro children sing Christmas carols in a kindergarten class in Washington D.C. These two pictures show the considerable difference between Africans and Americans of African descent. Today, many black Americans are, to some degree, of mixed ancestry.

ly from the mid-200's B.C. to the middle of the first century A.D. The rise of a rival state, Axum, to the southeast, caused Meroe's decline. In the next 1,000 years, several important states rose in western Africa. These trading nations, which became wealthy by exporting gold to the Muslim peoples of North Africa, included ancient Ghana, Kanem and Songhai.

In the 800's A.D., Muslim Arabs conquered North Africa. Most of the African rulers to the south became Muslims, in order to preserve or strengthen their trade with the Arabs. The African cities of Timbuctu and Jenne became noted centers of learning. Ghana's decline after 1076 was followed by the rise of Mali, under King Sundiata (1230-53). After Mali's decline in the early 1400's, Songhai, under Sonni Ali (1464-92), rose to become even greater. From the 1200's, similar though smaller states arose in the West African forest regions. Their art and culture, based probably on that of Nok, reached its finest development in the bronze (an alloy of copper and tin) sculptures of Ife and Benin.

In the mid-1400's, Portuguese traders from Europe arrived at Cape Verde and

This print shows a slave sale in Charleston, South Carolina, in 1856. The slave trade to the United States was abolished in 1808, but slavery itself was not abolished within America until the Civil War.

Important Events in Negro History

2000 B.C.	African peoples formed farming villages on grasslands south of the Sahara desert.
1000 B.C.	Trade began to develop between North and West Africa across the Sahara.
500 B.C.	Farming began in West African forest lands.
200's B.C.	Rise of ironworking kingdom of Meroe, in northeastern Africa. The Nok culture flourished in what is now Nigeria.
100's B.C.	Ironworking began in West Africa.
A.D. 300's	The kingdom of Axum conquered Meroe.
700's	Arabs, united by the Muslim religion, conquered North Africa.
750	Rise of Ancient Ghana (to the north of present-day Ghana); gold and salt were traded.
800	Muslim religion began to influence western Africa.
850	The Kanem empire of western Africa was founded.
1000	Ancient Ghana reached the height of its power. Timbuctu and Jenne were founded. Other west African tribes and states, including Hausa, Yoruba and Songhai, began to develop. Arabic arts and sciences flourished in North Africa.
1076	North African Almoravid Berbers captured the capital of Ancient Ghana, beginning the collapse of this empire.
1100's	Art flourished in the Yoruba state of Ife, in what is now Nigeria.
1200	Early Benin state established in what is now Nigeria.
1230	Rise of Mali empire under King Sundiata in western Africa.
1255	Rise of the Kanem empire in western Africa.
1375	Mali empire began to decline.
1415	Timbuctu and Jenne were noted West African centers of Muslim scholarship.
1444-5	Portuguese traders reached the West African coastlands.
1464	Rise of Songhai empire under King Sunni Ali.
1500's	The beginnings of the transatlantic slave trade to the Americas.
1590's	The Mali empire collapsed.
1600's	The Songhai empire collapsed. Dutch, British and French joined the slave trade.
1605	Escaped slaves in Brazil formed the kingdom of Palmares.
1650	Rise of Oyo empire in West Africa.
1694	Portuguese forces overthrew Palmares in Brazil.
1700's	Rise of the Asante empire in West Africa. Europeans in the West Indies made huge profits from sugar plantations worked by African slaves.
1775	The Benin empire declined.
1789	Revolution in France spread the ideal of liberty.
1791	Slave revolt in French West Indies led to the founding of the republic of Haiti. Freetown, capital of present-day Sierra Leone, was founded as a home for freed slaves.
1800	Gabriel Prosser led a slave revolt in Virgina.
1807	Slavery was abolished in the British empire.
1808	Slave trade to the United States was abolished.
1822	Denmark Vesey led a slave revolt in South Carolina.
1830's	Movement to abolish slavery began to grow in the United States.
1831	Nat Turner led a slave revolt in Virginia.
1847	Liberia, a colony settled in West Africa by freed slaves from the United States, declared itself a republic.
1861	Civil war broke out in the United States.
1863	Abraham Lincoln signed the Emancipation Proclamation to free slaves in the Confederacy.
1865	Congress passes 13th amendment to constitution to abolish slavery throughout United States.
1880's	European powers divided most of Africa into colonies.
1881	Booker T. Washington founded the Tuskegee Institute, Alabama, to educate Negroes.
1900	First Pan-African Conference held in London, England.
1910	National Association for Advancement of Colored People founded in the United States.
1916	Marcus Garvey founded a branch of his Universal Negro Improvement Association in the United States.
1920's	'Negro Renaissance' in the United States produced noted artists, musicians and scientists.
1930's	Nation of Islam founded in the United States.
1945	Sixth Pan-African Congress was held in Manchester, England.
1954	United States Supreme Court outlawed segregation in education.
1956	Bus boycott in Montgomery, Alabama, began a peaceful campaign for black civil rights.
1957	Ghana (formerly the Gold Coast) won its independence from Britain. It became the first black African nation to become independent.
1960	Student Non-Violent Coordinating Committee was formed in the United States to press for race equality. Seventeen colonies in Africa became independent nations.
1965	Assassination of Malcolm X, leading Black Muslim.
1968	Assassination of Dr Martin Luther King, the civil rights leader.

the mouth of the Senegal River on the West African coast. In the early 1500's, the Portuguese started to buy slaves from the rulers of the West African states, in exchange for firearms. In the 1600's, Portuguese were joined by English, Dutch and French traders. By the 1860's, when the trade finally ceased, millions of Africans had been transported to the New World. Through their forced labor they played an essential part in building up the countries of the Americas. In Africa, the trade did not destroy African society, but it distorted its development. Some African leaders wished to stop slavery, but the introduction of European firearms made it difficult. If one king refused to sell slaves, the Europeans would go to the next king. The first would then be threatened by the guns the other received for slaves. Therefore the trade continued. (See Slavery.)

However, once in the New World, many slaves gained freedom through rebellions or by escaping. In 1605, escaped slaves formed the kingdom of Palmares, in northeastern Brazil. It lasted until 1694, when Portuguese forces overthrew it. In the late 1700's, the slaves of the French Caribbean colony of St Domingue, led by Toussaint L'Ouverture, revolted and formed the republic of Haiti. In 1868, a general of African descent, Antonio Maceo, led the struggle for Cuba's independence.

In the United States in the 1700's and 1800's, free blacks (who had escaped from slavery or been freed by their owners) and slaves themselves helped shape the country's history. Crispus Attucks, an escaped slave, was one of the first American soldiers to die in the Revolutionary War. In the early 1800's, Gabriel Prosser,

Left: A carving in wood of a seated male figure, made by a Baule tribesman of Ivory Coast, Africa. African art has strongly influenced many European artists. Below: A meeting of the United Nations Security Council is addressed by a Ugandan delegate. With the gaining of independence by most African nations since World War II, Africa has become important in world politics.

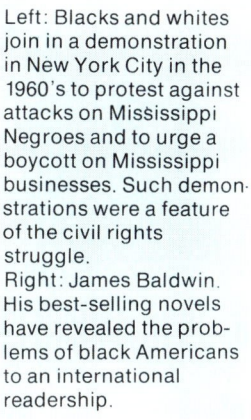

Left: Blacks and whites join in a demonstration in New York City in the 1960's to protest against attacks on Mississippi Negroes and to urge a boycott on Mississippi businesses. Such demonstrations were a feature of the civil rights struggle.
Right: James Baldwin. His best-selling novels have revealed the problems of black Americans to an international readership.

Denmark Vesey and Nat Turner led major slave revolts in the southern states. Free blacks, such as Paul Cuffe, a shipowner of Boston, Massachusetts, took part in the movement to 'colonize' West Africa with ex-slaves. This led to the foundation of Liberia (see Liberia). Blacks as well as whites figured prominently in the *abolitionist* movement to end slavery in the years before the American Civil War (see Abolitionists). Frederick Douglass, who escaped from slavery and became an influential journalist and speaker, was one of the most noted. Others were Josiah Henson, Sojourner Truth and Harriet Tubman. During the Civil War itself, black regiments fought alongside the northern forces.

In the *reconstruction* period that followed the Civil War, black people, supported by their white northern allies, held some power in the state governments of the South. However, in the later 1800's, when the northern support was removed, southern whites regained control and established laws to *segregate* (separate) the blacks from themselves and restrict their *civil rights*, especially the right to vote. In spite of this, progress was made in education under such leaders as Booker T. Washington. Other leaders pressed for black civil rights. One of the most important was W. E. B. DuBois, who in 1910 helped found the National Association for the Advancement of Colored People.

A major development of the early 1900's, particularly during World War I, was the movement of thousands of blacks from the South to the industrial cities of the North. This led to increased economic and educational progress for some blacks, and resulted in the 'Negro Renaissance' of the 1920's, in which many blacks became noted as writers, artists, scientists and musicians.

After World War II, pressure for full civil rights increased, and in 1954 the United States Supreme Court outlawed segregation in southern schools. During the following ten years, the Civil Rights movement, led by Martin Luther King Jr., pressed for peaceful *integration* and voting equality. The movement often met with violent resistance. The campaign for civil rights was carried on in the 1960's by the Student Non-Violent Coordinating Committee and other organizations. However, there had long been a section of black opinion that opposed integration and supported the idea of a separate, black nation. During the early 1900's, the leading figure in black nationalism was Marcus Garvey. From the early 1930's, the Nation of Islam, whose members practiced the Muslim faith, continued the nationalist movement. In the later 1960's, the Black Panther party turned to armed resistance to counter racial injustice.

The struggle of black people to achieve equality, particularly in the United States,

Martin Luther King Jr., perhaps the best-known black American leader of the 1950's and 60's, received the Nobel Peace Prize in 1964. In 1955, he successfully led a bus boycott in Montgomery, Alabama, to protest against discrimination against Negro passengers. In the next ten years, his policy of 'non-violent resistance' to racial injustice gained many white and black supporters and won major civil rights reforms. But even before his assassination in 1968, many black Americans had decided that a more aggressive approach to their problems was needed.

has given rise to increasing awareness and pride in their cultural heritage. At the insistence of black students, many colleges and universities have instituted Black Studies or 'Third World' Studies programs. The attainment of independence by most African countries and the growth of their influence in the 1960's (see Africa) have contributed to this development. Many American blacks, especially the young, see themselves as part of a separate culture within the United States.

Left: *Nelson and the Prize* by Richard Westall. This painting shows the young Nelson taking leave of his captain, Captain William Locker, to take command of a captured vessel with a heavy sea running. This was Nelson's first independent command.

Above: Nelson in the full dress uniform of a Vice-Admiral of the White Squadron. From a painting by L. F. Abbott.

Below: The Battle of Trafalgar. Nelson destroyed the combined fleets of France and Spain, but was mortally wounded at the height of the battle.

Nelson, Horatio (1758-1805), a British admiral, was one of the greatest seamen in history. His brilliant victories in several battles against the French made Britain a great sea power and crippled Napoleon's empire in Europe. He was a great leader because both the ordinary seamen and his officers trusted him and were trusted by him.

Nelson, the son of a rector, was born at the parsonage of Burnham Thorpe in Norfolk. He went to sea as a boy, soon deciding that he would be a hero. So rapid was his promotion that he was a post captain by the age of twenty. From 1793 onwards he was fighting the French and Spanish in the Mediterranean. For his outstanding tactics at the Battle of Cape St Vincent, 1797, under Admiral Jervis, he was acclaimed a hero by his countrymen. A wound made him blind in one eye, and the following year he lost his right arm in a daring attack on Santa Cruz de Tenerife in the Canary Isles. By this time he was a rear-admiral. He chased the French throughout the Mediterranean before completely defeating them at the Battle of the Nile in 1798.

Nelson was struck down by a shot while gaining his most famous victory—at Trafalgar. As commander-in-chief of the British fleet, he had pursued the French to the West Indies and back before cornering them at Cape Trafalgar, Spain, on October 21, 1805. The beginning of the great battle was marked by Nelson's famous signal: 'England expects that every man will do his duty.' Nelson died on his ship the *Victory* as the battle was ending.

Nelson's column in Trafalgar Square is one of the chief landmarks of London.

Nelson River This is the longest river in Manitoba, Canada. The source of the Nelson is the north end of Lake Winnipeg.

Below left: Nelson's flagship, the *Victory*, led the British fleet at the Battle of Trafalgar. Seen here in dry dock at Portsmouth, England, it is flying the signal 'England expects that every man will do his duty'.

Below right: An aerial view of the Grand Rapids power project on the Nelson River in Manitoba, Canada.

From this source it flows about 400 miles to the northeast, through lakes Playgreen, Cross and Split. It empties into Hudson Bay near Port Nelson. The river is an important source of hydroelectric power for the surrounding province.

The Nelson is part of a vast river system. The Saskatchewan River flows into the northwest end of Lake Winnipeg. Sometimes this whole system (Saskatchewan River-Lake Winnipeg-Nelson River) is called the Nelson River. The complete length of this waterway is 1,600 miles.

The first European to discover the Nelson was the English navigator Sir Thomas Button, who also named the river. Button was searching for the northwest passage, a trade route over the top of North America to the East. The river later became an important means of transportation for fur traders in the area, especially for Hudson's Bay Company.

Nepal This central Asian kingdom lies north of India and south of Tibet. It covers an area of 54,362 square miles and is a little larger than Arkansas.

The country's 10,210,000 people are mostly farmers of Mongolian, Indian or *Gurkha* (mixed) descent. Most of the people live in the fertile Nepal valley, in the central region. The main crops are rice, wheat and fruit. Only about one-tenth of the people live in cities and towns, where handicrafts are the main industries. The capital is Katmandu.

The Himalayan Mountains lie in northern Nepal. Mt Everest, the world's highest peak, is in Nepal. The country's climate ranges from mild conditions in the south to the bitter cold of the north.

Left: The map shows the location of the mountain kingdom of Nepal (marked in black). Below: A street scene in Katmandu, Nepal's capital and largest city. In the foreground, a porter brings wares from the countryside, and a hog searches for food.

Above: Neptune compared in size with the much smaller Earth. It is nearly 28,000 miles across.
Below: Through a telescope Neptune appears as a small greenish disc with lighter bands running across it.

Neptune Counting outwards from the Sun, Neptune is the eighth planet of the Solar System. It was discovered because irregular movements of Uranus led astronomers to suspect the presence of another planet nearby. They searched the probable area and eventually found Neptune in 1846.

Neptune is nearly 28,000 miles across. Its average distance from the Sun is 2,794 miles, and it takes 165 years to travel around it. The temperature on Neptune is about minus 330° F. Its atmosphere is a mixture of poisonous gases, probably about 2,000 miles deep. Its two moons are Triton and Nereid.

Netherlands The Netherlands is a small, low-lying country in western Europe. For its size, more people live there than in any other country—about 920 per square mile. The country is sometimes called Holland, and its people are known as Dutch.

The Netherlands is bounded on the north-west by the North Sea, on the east by Germany, and on the south by Belgium. It lies at the mouths of the Rhine, Maas (Meuse) and Scheldt (Schelde) rivers. Much of the land has been built up by silt dropped by the rivers where they enter the sea.

Nearly half the country is *polder* land —that is, land that has been reclaimed from the sea. Two-thirds of the polder land is below sea-level. It is protected from the sea by sand dunes and *dikes*, great banks built by the Dutch. The rest of the country is above sea-level, but the highest point is less than 350 feet.

The people speak Dutch, a language similar to German. Many Dutch people are tall, fair-haired and blue-eyed.

The principal ports are Rotterdam and Amsterdam. Although Amsterdam is the capital, the seat of government is at The Hague, an inland city where the International Court of Justice also sits.

Facts and Figures
Area: 15,785 square miles.
Population: 12,220,000.
Capital: Amsterdam.
Money Unit: guilder.
Labor force: 55% urban, 45% rural.
Exports: bulbs, dairy products, ships, textiles.
Imports: coffee, petroleum, tin, sugar.

Right: Cheeses and flower bulbs are among the Netherlands' chief exports. Below: The Netherlands is famous for its picturesque windmills.

Agriculture is very important since nearly all of the soil is rich and fertile. Dairying is more important than crop growing and the country exports large quantities of butter and cheese. Almost as important is the growing of tulip, hyacinth and other flower bulbs in the area around Haarlem.

Apart from petroleum and natural gas, the country has few natural resources.

Dutch industries process food or other agricultural products, such as flax and sugar. Engineering and chemical industries are also important. International trade passing through its ports to other European lands contributes to the Netherlands' wealth. Some goods travel along the network of canals that covers the country.

For hundreds of years the Netherlands and Belgium were linked together. They were often known as the Low Countries. The area came under the rule of Spain in the early 1500's. Fifty years later, the people of the Netherlands, led by William, Prince of Orange, rebelled against Spain, and formed a republic. War with Spain lasted until 1648.

The French conquered the Netherlands in 1795, but the country regained its independence in 1815, after the Napoleonic Wars. The Germans occupied the Netherlands from 1940 to 1945, during World War II. In 1957, the country joined the European Common Market, a trade alliance with five other countries.

Nevada is a state in the western United States. It is nicknamed the 'Silver State' after the large amounts of silver once mined there. It is also called the *Sagebrush State* because many of these gray-green plants cover the desert.

Nevada has a population of 449,000. After Alaska, it has the smallest population of any American state. Tourism is the main source of income for Nevada. The gambling resorts at Las Vegas and

A flock of sheep is driven across a stream in Nevada. Livestock raising is among Nevada's leading industries, and the state has millions of acres of pasture.

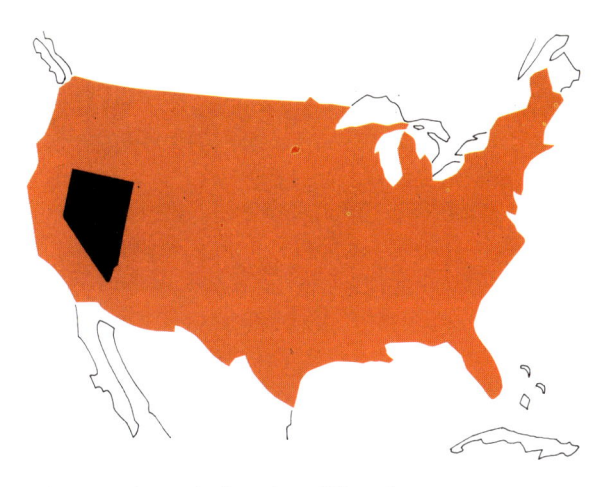

The map shows the location of Nevada.

Reno are world famous. Visitors also come to see ghost towns, such as Virginia City, that were once busy mining towns.

The state covers an area of 110,540 square miles. Most of Nevada lies within the Great Basin, a vast dry area that is mainly desert and plateau. There are also several mountain ranges. The highest point is Boundary Peak, 13,145 feet high, in southern Nevada. There are few lakes and rivers. The longest river, the Humboldt, flows about 300 miles through northern Nevada. Lake Tahoe, on the western border, is a popular resort. The only lake having an outlet to the sea is Lake Mead. This artificial lake was created when Hoover Dam was built.

Much of Nevada is suited to raising livestock. Crops grown include such cereals as alfalfa, barley, hay, oats, as well as wheat, potatoes and sugar beet. In the hottest areas, almonds, figs and grapes are also grown. Mineral resources include antimony, copper, gold, lead, manganese, mercury, silver, tungsten and zinc. Mining is still a chief industry in Nevada.

In 1859 silver was discovered at Comstock Lode, in Mt Davidson, western Nevada. Many settlers arrived, and Nevada was proclaimed a state on October 31, 1864. In the same year, Carson City was made the capital. When the price of silver fell in the 1870's and 1880's many people left. Livestock became increasingly important. In the 1900's more minerals were discovered, and the economy improved.

Atomic weapons are tested at the Nevada Test Site, northwest of Las Vegas.

New Amsterdam was the original name of New York. Established by the Dutch in 1626, the settlement was named Fort Amsterdam, after Amsterdam in the Netherlands. In the same year, the Dutch governor, Peter Minuit, bought the island of Manhattan from the Indians for about $24 worth of goods. As the settlement spread, the whole area came to be known as New Amsterdam, and was incorporated as a city in 1653. The Dutch and English were fighting at that time, and the city was finally taken over by the English in 1664, who changed its name (see New York City).

New Brunswick is one of Canada's four Atlantic provinces. It is situated on the border of the United States. The province was named after the British royal family of Brunswick-Lüneburg and has always had strong connections with Europe. Its popular name, the Loyalist Province, has its origin in the time when thousands of United Empire Loyalists (people who wished to remain loyal to England) left the United States to settle in New Brunswick after the Revolutionary War.

The province covers an area of 28,354 square miles. It has a temperate climate

The map shows the location (marked in black) of the Canadian Atlantic province of New Brunswick.

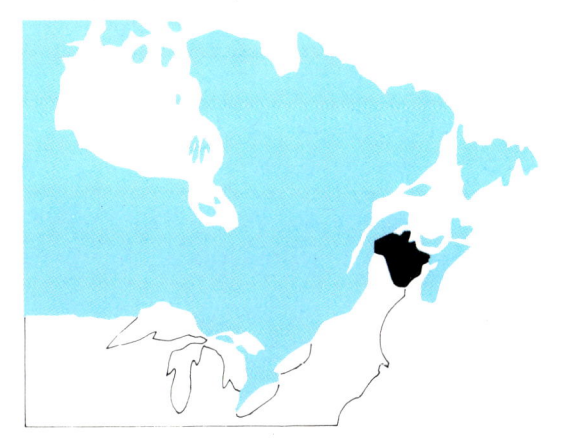

and forests cover much of the country. Through the forests, several rivers flow down to the sea. These rivers carry millions of logs yearly down to the paper and pulp mills on the coast. The most important industry is lumber. In the northeastern part of the province, rich resources of copper, lead, silver, and zinc were discovered in the 1950's and these minerals are now extensively mined. In most parts, the soil is infertile, but the rich land around the St John River Valley yields potatoes and apples. Dairy products and poultry are also important.

The capital, Fredericton, is situated in south-central New Brunswick on the St John River. The largest city and the leading commercial and industrial center is St John, which lies on the south coast. Half of New Brunswick's population of 624,000 live in rural areas. About one-sixth live in the metropolitan area of St John and about one-third in other cities.

New Brunswick is one of the best fishing and hunting grounds in North America and many tourists visit the province.

The known history of the province began with the arrival of French explorers in the 1500's and early 1600's. Later, it became a center of the fur trade, and in 1755, after wars against the French colonists, the British captured the region. In 1867 New Brunswick became one of the original four provinces of the Dominion of Canada.

New England The six states which form the area known since early times as New England are Maine, Vermont, New Hampshire, Massachusetts, Connecticut and Rhode Island. The region is situated with the Atlantic at its eastern border and Canada to its north. It is the northeasternmost part of the United States.

New England was named, appropriately, by an English seaman, Captain John Smith, in 1614 (see Smith, John). He felt

A peaceful landscape in Vermont, New England. This region contains much beautiful scenery.

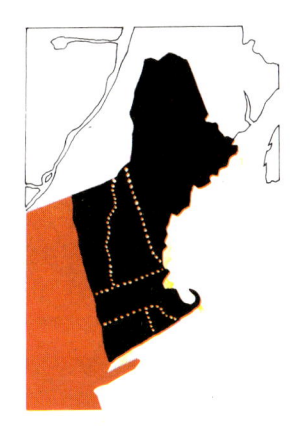

The map shows the location of the New England states, the northeasternmost region of the United States. It consists of Maine, Vermont, New Hampshire, Massachusetts, Connecticut and Rhode Island.

that its climate and much of its country resembled that of England, where most of the early settlers, such as the Pilgrim Fathers, came from.

New England was one of the earliest centers of American culture. It was also the main source of the national sentiment that brought about the Revolutionary War. It was often called the hotbed of American Revolution, and events such as the Boston Tea Party testify to its great involvement.

The largest city of New England is Boston, Massachusetts. About one-fourth of the total population of the area live within Boston's metropolitan area. The city is a leading cultural, financial and manufacturing center. Manufacturing industries are the source of most of the area's income. Products include electronic equipment, glass and leather, machinery and textiles.

Tourists are attracted by New England's invigorating climate, historical associations and beautiful landscapes. The jazz festival at Newport, Rhode Island, has become a major annual event and numerous coastal resorts provide entertainment and interest.

In early times, New Englanders were known for the qualities derived from their puritan ancestors, and for the response to the challenge which the new country presented. Famous New Englanders include statesmen, such as John Adams and Daniel Webster, and writers, such as Emily Dickinson, Ralph Waldo Emerson, Nathaniel Hawthorne, Henry James and Henry Wadsworth Longfellow.

Newfoundland is a province of Canada. Its island territories were once an independent dominion (see Canada). The province consists of the island of Newfoundland, off the Atlantic coast of Canada and Labrador, on the mainland. The total area is 156,183 square miles.

The coast of the island is rocky, with many deep inlets. The central part is a rugged plateau, with many lakes and forests. The forests provide timber for wood-pulp and paper-making, one of Newfoundland's main industries. The island is rich in minerals, including gypsum, iron ore, lead and zinc. Only a small amount of land around the coast can be farmed. The climate is cool, with several months of heavy snow in winter.

Labrador consists of a plateau sloping steeply to the coast, which has many *fjords* (deep sea inlets). Only about 10,000 of Newfoundland's 519,000 people live in Labrador. About one-third of the land is covered with forests. In the northwest lies one of the world's richest deposits of iron ore. The climate is generally colder than that of Newfoundland.

Fishing is one of the province's main industries. Near the island lie shallow areas of sea known as the Banks, where there is abundant food for fish. About 200 million cod are caught there every year. St. John's, Newfoundland's capital, is the base for the fishing fleet.

Newfoundland was Britain's oldest colony. It was claimed in 1583. It became self-governing in 1855, but after an economic crisis, sought help from Britain in 1934. It joined Canada in 1949.

New Guinea, one of the world's largest islands, lies in the tropics north of Australia. The western part of the island, West Irian, is part of Indonesia. Eastern New Guinea is divided into Papua and the United Nations Trust Territory of New Guinea. Australia governs both.

New Guinea has an area of 317,115 square miles. As an island, it is second only to Greenland in size.

The island has a 'backbone' of mountains from west to east. The mountains slope southwards to the southern plain, the western part of which is a tropical swamp. Except in the mountains, New Guinea is unpleasantly hot and humid. Forests cover much of the island.

The climate and physical features have made life difficult for the people of New Guinea and delayed the development of the island.

The population of New Guinea is about 2,500,000. Melanesian, Micronesian, Polynesian and pygmy people live in the island. The principal cities are Port Moresby and Sukarnapura, but they are both small.

About 700 languages and dialects are spoken and many religions practiced. Some islanders are Christians. Some follow a cult, called the *Cargo Cult,* that was inspired by the islanders' experiences in World War II. They wait for the return of huge birds (aircraft) to drop from the skies all the goods that the islanders want to possess. They believe that Europeans will then leave New Guinea, but leave their goods behind, as often happened during the war.

Spanish sailors landed in northern New Guinea in 1527. In 1660, the Dutch occupied part of western New Guinea. By the late 1880's, Britain and Germany shared the eastern part of the island. By 1920 Australia governed all eastern New Guinea. Northern New Guinea was occupied by the Japanese during World War II, and fierce fighting took place there. The Dutch handed over western New Guinea to Indonesia in 1963.

New Hampshire, a New England state, is largely rural, with a population of only 723,000. Forests cover nearly four-fifths of its area of 9,304 square miles. Its surface is rugged with a middle region of uplands and hills. New Hampshire's White Mountains are famed for their skiing. The Connecticut River forms the western boundary and supplies much of the state's electricity. Each summer, many people

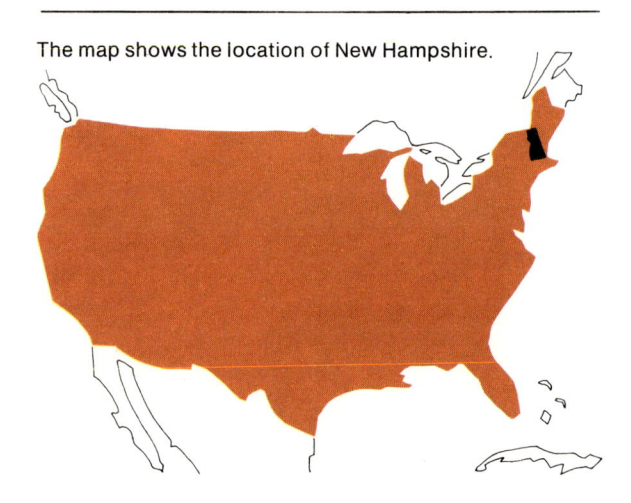

Below: Tribesmen from New Guinea and Papua, elaborately costumed with feather headdresses, prepare to enter the arena at the Mount Hagen show. The show was originated by New Guinea's Australian administrators. Bottom: Barakau, a village built on stilts, lies on the Papuan coast at the southeastern coast of New Guinea.

The map shows the location of New Hampshire.

from the large cities of the eastern United States visit New Hampshire, where the air and water are cleaner than in many other areas.

There is little farming in the rocky soil of New Hampshire. Most of the state's income comes from manufacturing. For more than 100 years New Hampshire has had an important leather industry, and shoes are one of its most important products. A major shipyard is at Portsmouth, on the tiny 15 miles of the state's Atlantic coast. Manchester is the major industrial city, and Concord is the state capital.

New Hampshire's present is closely linked with its past. More than 200 small, quiet villages are still governed by town meetings, where local laws and problems can be discussed by all who attend. The rural architecture of rectangular, undecorated wooden buildings has changed little in two hundred years. In the play *Our Town*, Thornton Wilder, one of

Two fishermen enjoy a peaceful day on a New Hampshire lake surrounded by brilliant autumn foliage.

America's famous dramatists, described life in a New Hampshire village.

The original settlers of New Hampshire included religious groups, who had to fight both the bitter New England winter and hostile Indians. New Hampshire was the first colony to declare independence from Britain in 1776. Later, it contributed men and materials to the North during the Civil War and was a fierce anti-slave state. Dartmouth College, an old educational institution, is in Hanover, New Hampshire.

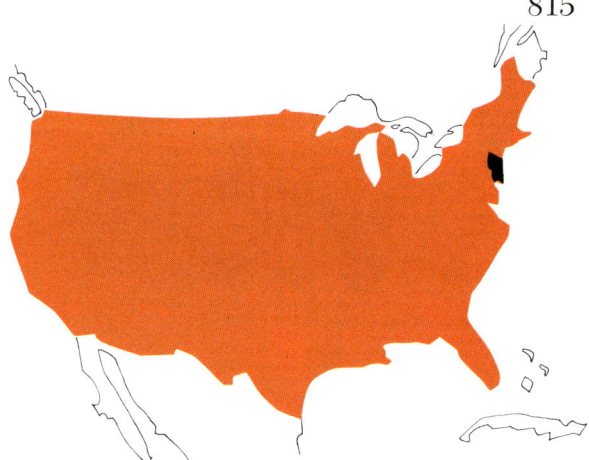

The map shows the location of New Jersey.

New Jersey is one of the most densely populated of the Middle Atlantic States, with 7,090,000 people living in an area of 7,836 square miles. More than half the state rests on a low, coastal plain, stretching inland from the Atlantic Ocean, New Jersey's long coastline and the northwestern section of Appalachian forests attract city dwellers during the summer. Atlantic City, a vacation and convention center, lies in the southern part of the state. Here, the Army Corps of Engineers has built jetties to save the state's beaches from being washed away.

New Jersey lies between the two major urban areas of New York and Philadelphia. This makes it partly a commuter or 'bedroom' area in which people live, although they travel each day to work in the large cities outside the state. New Jersey is a transportation center, criss-crossed by railroads and modern highways. There are major ocean ports at Hoboken and Newark. Large ships sail up the Delaware River, the State's western boundary. Newark Airport, which serves New York, is one of the busiest in the country.

New Jersey is largely a manufacturing state. Businesses and factories are attracted by the low state taxes. Chemicals are the major product. Farming is limited in this crowded state, employing less than 2 percent of the population. The Atlantic coastline yields an annual catch of shellfish. Historic universities are located at Princeton and Rutgers.

The Italian, Giovanni da Verrazano, was among the first Europeans to explore New Jersey, which later became one of the original thirteen English colonies. The western part of the state was settled by Quakers. For a while, the harbor at Perth Amboy rivaled New York. After the Revolutionary War, the state underwent rapid industrial growth and opened America's first railroad. Woodrow Wilson served as New Jersey's governor before becoming president in 1913. During World War II, the state was a troop transport area.

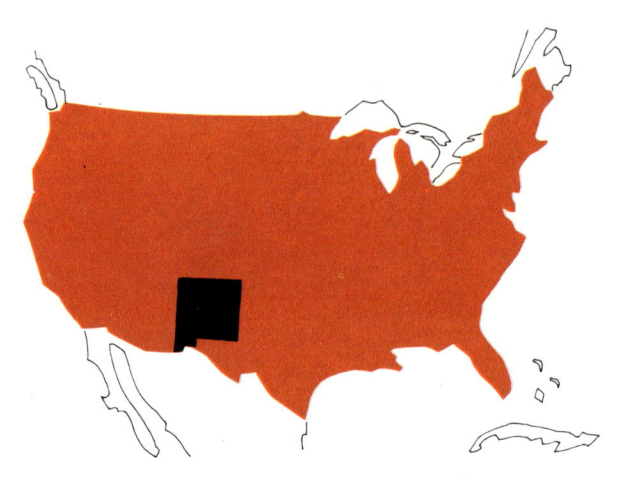

The map shows the location of New Mexico.

New Mexico is a large, thinly populated state on the Mexican border. It covers an area of 121,666 square miles and is the fifth largest state. However, it has only 999,000 people and ranks 36th in order of population. Much of New Mexico is covered with canyons, deserts and mountain ranges.

The state borders Arizona, Colorado, Oklahoma and Texas. To the south it borders Mexico. Down its center from north to south flows the Rio Grande which, helped by dams, irrigates a large part of the country. The Great Plains cover the eastern part of New Mexico. In the north-central area are the Rocky Mountains. The Basin and Range region, containing mountains and desert basins, covers the south and west. The broken Colorado plateau is in the northwest.

Mining and farming are the leading industries. Petroleum and natural gas are the chief products, but New Mexico also has important deposits of uranium and potash. New Mexican farms are large ranches where sheep and cattle graze. Crops are raised in irrigated areas.

The state capital is Santa Fe but the largest city is Albuquerque. Both cities are centrally situated. Albuquerque is on the Rio Grande, and Santa Fe lies near the river.

New Mexico attracts tourists because of its dramatic and rugged landscape, and because of its history. Remains of ancient settlements show that the state had an Indian civilization long before the discovery of America by Europeans. Spanish explorers claimed the region for Spain in the 1500's. In the 1800's, New Mexico became a province of Mexico. The United States took the region in the Mexican War of 1846-48. Clashes followed with Indian tribes. Colorful characters who contributed to New Mexico's turbulent history include Kit Carson and Billy the Kid. New Mexico became the 47th state of the Union in 1912. The culture of New Mexico still shows much Mexican and Spanish influence and the Spanish language is widely used. Mexican foods are a special feature.

New Orleans (pop. 585,787) is a city, seaport and former capital of Louisiana. Known as the birthplace of jazz, the city is located on low-lying marshland on the Mississippi delta, 107 miles from the river mouth on the Gulf of Mexico. A series of *levees* (embankments) are a feature of the riverside as a protection against flood. New Orleans is the largest city of Louisiana and the chief commercial center of the Gulf States.

New Orleans was founded in 1718 by the French under Bienville, and has risen to become the great cotton market of America and one of the foremost cotton ports of the world.

Newspapers provide us with news and comment and articles of interest every day. Daily papers are published every morning or evening in a superbly organized rush of activity. About 300 million daily newspapers are sold throughout the world every day. A third of these are printed in English. The United States and Russia have the highest *circulation* (sales) of newspapers—about 60 million copies per day. But the Swedes are the world's most avid newspaper readers. In Sweden, about one person in two buys a daily newspaper. Newspapers are also published weekly. Sunday newspapers are popular, and about 50 million of these papers are sold in the United States every week. The circulation of other American weekly papers amounts to about 25 million.

The first newspaper to be published in the United States was *Publick Occurrences Both Foreign and Domestic*. The first issue, which was also the last, appeared in Boston on September 25, 1690. Now there are about 1,750 daily newspapers in the United States and about 8,200 weekly and semiweekly papers. Most American newspapers concentrate on giving news of the region in which they are published, and they are bought only in that region.

In Britain and Russia several daily newspapers are read nationally. Britain has nine national dailies and Russia two. One of Russia's, *Pravda* (meaning *truth*), has one of the largest circulations of any newspaper—5 million copies a day.

In some countries, including Greece, Russia and Spain, newspapers are controlled by governments. In other countries, a newspaper may print what it likes.

Newts are amphibian animals which can live both in fresh water and on the land. Newts have long tails to swim with and four short legs to move about on land.

The front page of the *Times*, for long one of Britain's leading newspapers, contains the news of the victory at Trafalgar in November, 1805. Newspapers began to appear regularly during the 1700's.

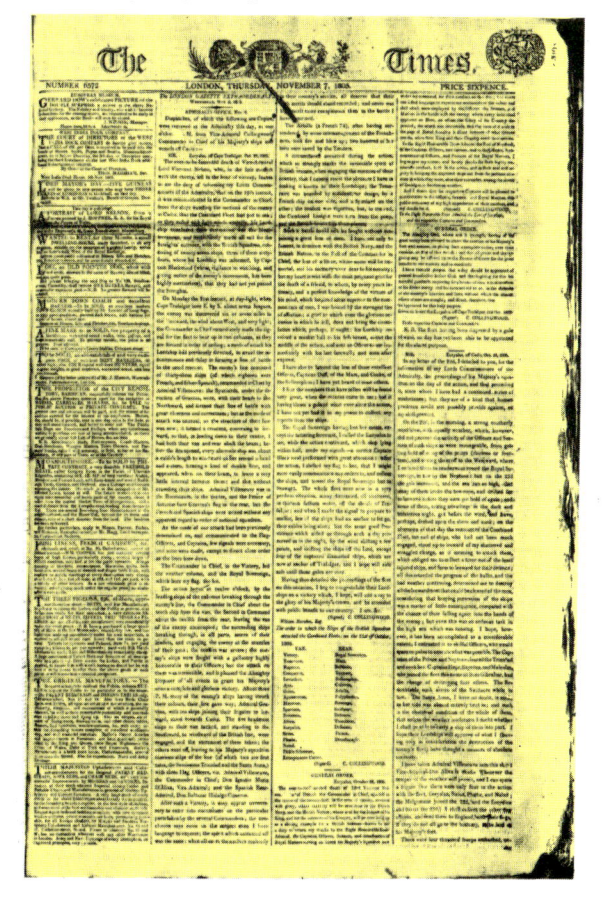

A typical scene in the French Quarter of New Orleans.

A newt is also called an *eft*. Newts are related to salamanders, and, like salamanders, many newts are brightly colored. (See Amphibians.)

Newts are cold-blooded animals and hibernate through the winter. They breed in the spring, laying eggs singly on water plants in ponds. The eggs hatch to form tadpoles. These develop like the tadpoles of frogs except that the newt tadpole does not lose its tail (see Frog). Some newt tadpoles never leave the water, and breed without reaching complete adulthood. Most newts spend much time in the water. Like frogs, they can breathe by absorbing oxygen from the water through their skin. But in the summer they usually leave the water to live in moist places on the land.

Newts grow to a length of about three to six inches. They are unusual in that they can grow new legs to replace any they lose.

Newton, Sir Isaac (1642-1727), was an English mathematician who made outstanding contributions to the study of physics. His theories of gravity and motion and experiments in light physics, have earned him a place among the most celebrated of scientists.

As a boy he was not a notable scholar. Neither did he show great ability while studying at Trinity College, Cambridge. However his greatest discoveries were made during a period of only two years, soon after leaving college.

Newton proved that sunlight is made up of all the colors of the rainbow. He demonstrated this by passing sunlight through a *prism* (a triangular block of glass) onto a piece of paper. This resulted in the *spectrum,* or band of colors, being clearly seen. To prove conclusively that his theory was correct, Newton then passed the spectrum back through another prism and obtained white light again. Although similar theories had previously been put forward, it was Newton who proved it beyond doubt.

It is popularly believed that Newton's theories of motion and gravity came to him when he saw an apple fall from a tree to the ground beneath. *Gravity* is the attraction that masses of matter have for each other, and *motion* occurs when an object changes its position in space. Newton reasoned that the force with which the Earth attracts an object depends on the amount of *matter* (of which all physical things are made) in the object, and the distance between them. Therefore a large stone will be attracted to earth by a greater force than a small stone. Newton also concluded that the planets are held in their orbits by the gravitational pull of the Sun, while the Moon is held in its orbit by the Earth's gravitational pull.

It was nearly twenty years later that Newton's theories were published. The resulting book is considered one of the most important of all scientific works. His work on the laws of motion became the basis for the science of mechanics.

Newton had an extremely busy academic and public life. In 1669 he was appointed professor of mathematics at Cambridge, and later became the university's member of parliament. He also became Master of the Mint and President of the Royal Society. Newton was knighted by Queen Anne in 1705. He is buried in Westminster Abbey in London.

A male Smooth Newt (above), and a female Warty Newt (below).

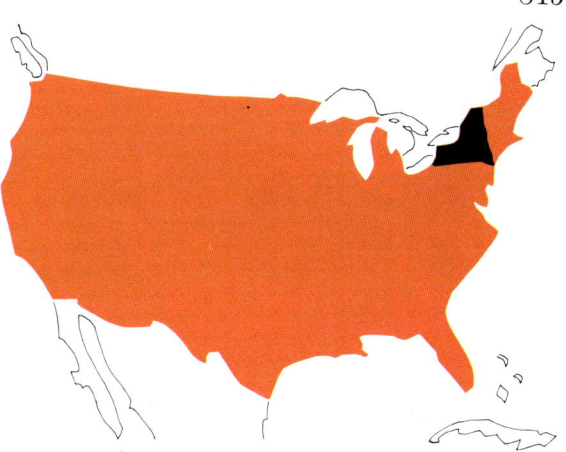

819

The map shows the location (marked in black) of New York State.

Above: Isaac Newton. Below: The Eastman Kodak plant at Rochester is one of New York's many industrial plants.

New York covers an area of 49,576 square miles and ranks 30th among the states in order of size. With its population of 17,980,000, however, it is the second most populated state. Only California, which covers more than three times the area of New York, has a larger population. More than half of the people of New York live in or around New York

A view of the lighthouse at Montauk Point on the eastern tip of Long Island, in New York State. Although much of Long Island's countryside has become thickly populated, there are still numerous summer resorts along the island's wooded northern shore.

City, the largest city in the United States and one of the largest in the world.

About 85 people out of every 100 in New York State live in cities and towns. Besides New York City, the state has other great cities, including Albany, the state capital, Buffalo, Rochester, Syracuse, Yonkers and Niagara Falls. About one-sixth of the population of the state was born outside the United States. They include people of Italian, German, Irish, Russian, Polish and Puerto Rican origin.

New York State is the industrial and business center of the United States. Its most important industries include clothing, electrical machinery, food processing, printing and publishing. The harbor of New York City is the leading seaport in the United States. Buffalo, on Lake Erie, has become increasingly important as a port since the opening of the St Lawrence Seaway in 1959. New York State has been the leading manufacturing state since the 1830's and, because of its wealth, it gained the nickname 'The Empire State'.

Only about 4 people out of every 100 in New York work on farms. However, agriculture is still an important source of income. The state has excellent pasture land and dairy farming is a major occupation. Milk, butter and other dairy products are the leading farm products in New York. Poultry farming and beef cattle raising are also important.

Many tourists visit New York State. Some are attracted by the sights of New York City (see New York City). Outside the cities, however, there are many scenic areas. The rugged Adirondack Mountains in the northeastern part of the state offer climbing and skiing facilities. The state also contains thousands of lakes, and many waterfalls and rivers. Niagara Falls in the west is especially popular. The Catskill Mountains and the Hudson Valley are popular tourist areas in the east and

Long Island has fine beaches. The state also has many places of historic interest, including the Saratoga National Park and West Point. The Statue of Liberty National Monument is in New York Bay, and the Castle Clinton National Monument, the historic landing depot for immigrants, is in New York harbor.

New York was one of the original 13 states. It adopted its first state constitution in 1777. It was first claimed for Holland by Henry Hudson, an Englishman employed by the Dutch East India Company, in 1609. The Dutch named it *New Netherland*. When the English took over in 1664, they changed the name to New York, after the English Duke of York. During the Revolutionary War (1775-1783), New York was the scene of many battles. From 1785 to 1790, New York City was the first capital of the United States. In the 1800's, New York expanded production until it led all other states.

New York City is a city and seaport of the state of New York, in the eastern United States. It is located on three islands and a part of the mainland at the mouth of the Hudson (or North) River at the head of New York Bay.

Originally a small Dutch settlement at the southern tip of Manhattan Island, the city now incorporates the five boroughs of Manhattan, Brooklyn, Queens, Richmond (Staten Island), and Bronx (mainland). With a population of 7,975,000, it is the largest city in the western hemisphere and after Tokyo and London the third largest in the world. Huge bridges and long tunnels crossing the Hudson and East Rivers are of major importance in the city's communications.

It is the chief commercial center of the United States, with Manhattan the commercial and financial heart of the city. Mammoth skyscrapers are a feature of the city. The Empire State Building, long the world's tallest building, is exceeded in

New York. The United Nations building (right foreground).

height only by the new World Trade Center in downtown Manhattan, near the New York Stock Exchange, the greatest securities market in the world. The city is the headquarters of many industrial concerns, and major industries include textiles, publishing, iron and steel works, machinery manufacture, sugar refining and chemical products.

New York is the principal port of America. The west side of Manhattan Island on the Hudson River is lined with docks and port facilities, and there are also important docks at Brooklyn. One of the largest harbors in the world, it carries more than half the total foreign trade of the United States. The waters of the Hudson River, East River, Long Island Sound, and the Harlem River are used extensively by small freighter and barge traffic.

The city is an important educational and cultural center and is the seat of Columbia University (founded 1754), of the New York University (1831) and of many other academic institutions. The New York Public Library is one of the largest in the world, with more than 80 miles of bookshelves.

New Zealand is a country over 1,000 miles south-east of Australia. Most of New Zealand is made up of two large islands, called North Island and South Island. It contains several other islands, but they are very small. New Zealand is almost as big as the British Isles. More than nine-tenths of all New Zealanders were born in the British Isles, or are descended from British and Irish people who settled in New Zealand.

North Island, where two-thirds of all New Zealanders live, extends about 500 miles from north to south. Its low mountains and hills include two active volcanoes. South Island is separated from North Island by the 16-mile-wide Cook Strait. From the Strait, the Southern Alps stretch south-westwards for more than 500 miles throughout the island. New Zealand's highest mountain, Mount Cook, rises from this range.

Several bays and beaches lie along New Zealand's 4,300-mile-long coastline. The country has several rivers. Most of them flow so swiftly down steep slopes that boats cannot use them. New Zealand has many scenic lakes and waterfalls. In addition to active volcanoes, New Zealand has other natural features associated with volcanic activity. On North Island is a region where hot springs and boiling mud pools are found. Some of the hot springs are *geysers*, which periodically shoot up a tall column of hot water and steam.

New Zealand has a mild climate. In January the country's mid-summer temperature averages about 68° F (20° C). In July, temperatures drop to about 42° F (6° C). Rainfall is very varied, averaging between 20 and 200 inches in various parts of the islands.

New Zealand has several species of rare

Facts and Figures
Area: 103,736 square miles.
Population: 2,781,000.
Capital: Wellington.
Money Unit: New Zealand dollar.
Labor force: 36% rural; 64% urban.
Exports: butter, cheese, meat, wool.
Imports: fuel, machinery, textiles, tools.

Sheep-farming is vital to New Zealand's economy. Wool and lamb are among its chief exports.

birds. The tail-less kiwi is often used as a symbol for the country.

About 7 people out of every 100 are *Maoris*, who are descendants of the Polynesian people who sailed to the islands about 700 years ago. Many marriages have occurred between Maoris and Europeans. The official language of New Zealand is English, but the Maoris also have their own language. The religion of the country is Christianity.

New Zealand is one of the most prosperous countries in the world. It was one of the earliest countries to introduce social reforms and a social security system, including old age pensions. The mild climate allows New Zealanders to enjoy much outdoor life in their leisure time, to a far greater extent than their parents or grandparents did in Britain. Popular recreation includes athletics, cricket and rugby football. Most New Zealanders live in small towns or villages. Only Auckland, Christchurch, Dunedin and Wellington, the capital, have more than 100,000 people.

Half of New Zealand's area is farmland, and the country exports butter, lamb, fruit and other food products, especially to Britain. New Zealand has fertile soil. Farmers grow grains for consumption within the country. Because the most modern methods of farming are used, only a sixth of the country's people work on the land. Two-thirds of the people work in manufacturing and processing industries of various kinds. Much electrical power comes from hydroelectric plants, which harness the power of New Zealand's rushing rivers. The fishing industry is also important but employs few people.

Forests cover about a fifth of New Zealand. Most of the forests were planted in the 1920's. The country's mineral wealth includes coal, iron ore, gold, limestone, natural gas, silver and tungsten.

Road, rail, sea and air transport is good in New Zealand, and almost every

Above: Maoris in national costume perform an action song. The Maoris inhabited New Zealand when the first settlers arrived.
Above center: The cathedral at Christchurch, on South Island.
Far right: A climbing party negotiates an icebridge in Mt. Cook National Park. New Zealanders are fond of outdoor recreations. 
Below right: Hot springs at Rotorua. This area is famous for its geysers of boiling mud pools.
Left: The kiwi is a tailless, flightless bird which is often used as a national emblem.

family has a car. Geographically remote from other countries, New Zealand has good air and sea connections with the rest of the world.

New Zealand is a monarchy. It has the same queen, Elizabeth II, as Britain. In New Zealand, the Queen is represented by a governor-general. The government is headed by a prime minister. He and his cabinet are members of the elected House of Representatives, the nation's parliament.

The earliest-known people in New Zealand were Morioris — a Polynesian people. They were conquered in about the 1300's by another Polynesian people, Maoris, who settled mainly on the coastal parts of North Island.

Abel Tasman, commander of a ship sailing for the Dutch East India Company, sighted New Zealand in 1642. The Dutch named the islands after Zeeland, a province in the Netherlands. The Dutch kept their discovery secret. James Cook, a British sea captain, found and charted the island in 1769. But the British took little interest in the country for the next 70 years.

In 1839, Edward Gibbon Wakefield, a British statesman, who had formed a New Zealand Company, sent a group of British colonists to settle on the islands. The first colonists settled at Wellington. To protect them, the British government incorporated New Zealand into their Australian colony of New South Wales.

In 1840, Maori chiefs signed a treaty accepting British rule, and in 1841 New Zealand became a colony independent of Australia. Disputes about land led to war between the Maoris and the settlers in 1845-1848. Fighting occurred again in the 1860's and 1870's.

In 1907, New Zealand became an independent dominion within the British empire. Its troops fought in Europe in both World Wars. More recently New Zealand has sent troops into Vietnam to support the Australian and United States forces.

Niagara Falls are two waterfalls that occur in the Niagara River, on the borders of the United States and Canada. The Niagara River is a short river that connects Lake Erie with Lake Ontario. All the Great Lakes except for Lake Ontario empty into it. Goat Island divides the river just before the falls.

The falls themselves are set in beautiful scenery, and are a favorite resort for tourists, especially honeymooners. Half a million tons of water a minute fall

Above: Niagara Falls. In the foreground is an observation tower overlooking the Horseshoe Falls.

Left: In 1859 Charles Blondin crossed Niagara on a tightrope. He subsequently repeated this feat carrying a man on his back.

into a steep gorge. The larger of the two streams falls on the Canadian side as the Horseshoe Falls. They are 158 feet high and 2,600 feet wide at their widest point. The American Falls are formed by the smaller stream. They are 167 feet high and about 1,000 feet wide. During the winter the falls sometimes freeze into a curtain of ice.

Many power plants have been installed near the falls to use their tremendous water power.

Nicaragua is a Central American republic. It covers an area of 53,938 square miles and is bordered by Honduras in the north and by Costa Rica in the south. There are three main regions: the forested, hot, rainy Caribbean lowlands; the high, cool Central highlands; and the Pacific lowlands.

Most of the 1,800,000 people live in the fertile Pacific coastlands. The people are mainly *mestizos*, people of mixed European and Indian origin. The chief crops include coffee, cotton and sugar. The capital and largest city, Managua, is located in the Pacific region. The Central highlands are the second most important farming region. Managua is the main industrial center and leading products include processed foods and clothing.

The area that is now Nicaragua was discovered by Christopher Columbus in 1502. For about 300 years, control of the area passed from Spain to England and other European powers. Nicaragua became completely independent in 1838.

The map shows the location (marked in black) of the Central American republic of Nicaragua.

A nickel concentration plant at Kambalda, Australia. Nickel is among the world's most useful metals.

Nickel is used widely in the form of plating and in alloys. It is electroplated on metals such as steel to protect them from corrosion. (See Electroplating.) Nickel is added with chromium to steel to make it stainless. With copper, nickel forms a wide range of alloys, including the cupronickel used for 'silver' coinage and the nickel-silver used for cutlery. With chromium, nickel forms heat-resistant alloys which are used in jet engines and electric fires. Nickel is also used in nickel-iron and nickel-cadmium batteries.

The main nickel ore is pentlandite. About half the world's nickel comes from Ontario, Canada. Nickel is also found in Australia, Brazil, Cuba, Indonesia, the USSR and the United States.

Nigeria, in western Africa, has the largest population of any African country. But 12 other African countries cover a larger area. The country is named after the long River Niger, which flows into the sea through a vast swampy delta.

The land varies from steaming-hot tropical forests and swamps in the south, to grassland merging into desert in the north. In the south, the rainfall reaches more than 150 inches a year. In the far north, the average rainfall may be below 20 inches a year.

The four main groups of people are the Hausa and Fulani of the north, the Yoruba of the south-west, and the Ibo of the south-east. The Yoruba and Ibo are Negro people, but the Muslim Hausa and Fulani are Hamitic, a brown-skinned people with narrow noses and thin lips.

The cities of Nigeria are modern and most city-dwellers wear western dress. But many people wear colorful robes decorated with traditional patterns. In the villages, people still live in mud houses with thatched or corrugated iron roofs. About half the peole are Muslims, and about a quarter are Christians. The others follow tribal religions.

Farming is Nigeria's chief industry. Important crops include cocoa, groundnuts (peanuts), palm kernels and palm oil. Tin and columbite are mined.

Nigeria was the home of several African civilizations, which produced some of the finest African art. The greatest cultures were the Nok culture of the 200's B.C., the Ife culture of the A.D. 1100's, and the Benin culture which lasted from the 1200's until the 1770's. British influence in Nigeria began in the 1700's. From 1906, Britain ruled the entire country.

Nigeria gained independence in 1960 and became a republic in 1963. In 1966, army officers overthrew the elected government. In 1967, the people of south-eastern Nigeria rebelled and established their own state of Biafra. The central government did not recognize Biafra and a long and terrible civil war began. The war continued until the collapse of Biafra in January 1970.

Above: A typical Nigerian market scene.

Left: The map shows the location of Nigeria (marked in black).

Facts and Figures
Area: 356,669 square miles.
Population: 60,500,000.
Capital: Lagos.

Nightingale, Florence (1820-1910), completely changed people's attitude towards nursing in the 1800's. She organized care for wounded British soldiers in the Crimean War in Turkey and was the first woman to give good hospital care to soldiers fighting outside their own country. Soldiers called Florence 'the lady with the lamp', because she walked through their hospital wards at night and the light from her lamp was a symbol of her care.

Left: A portrait of Florence Nightingale, the 'Lady with the Lamp' Above: Scutari, where many of the British wounded from the Crimean war were taken, was a converted Turkish barracks. Florence Nightingale transformed it into an efficient hospital.

Florence Nightingale was born near Florence, in Italy, where her wealthy parents were living. She spent most of her early life in England. She took an interest in helping other people, especially if they were ill. She studied nursing, and at 33 took charge of a London hospital.

The British became angry when they learned that wounded British soldiers fighting in the Crimea had no proper care. Florence Nightingale went to the Crimea to take charge of nursing the wounded soldiers. She left England with 38 nurses.

The problems Florence faced were enormous, but she proved to be a brilliant organizer. She made sure the hospital was clean, and she made the government send supplies. She worked very hard, and nearly died from fever. But she recovered and stayed until the end of the war.

When she returned, she went quietly home and then moved to London to continue her nursing studies. The strain of overwork made her an invalid, but for the rest of her life she continued her efforts to improve nursing care.

Nile The Nile is a river of north-eastern Africa, and flows 4,160 miles from its source in the great lakes of central Africa to its wide delta on the Mediterranean. The largest of the Nile's tributaries is the Blue Nile, which rises in the mountains of Ethiopia.

The Nile Valley and Delta, where the Nile widens out through channels to the Mediterranean, forms a long narrow oasis through the burning-hot desert belt of North Africa. This fertile river valley is part of Egypt, and is highly cultivated and thickly populated. An area of over a million square miles is irrigated by the river and delta of the Nile. A series of huge dams controls the waters of the Nile, which flood down in spring and early summer from the mountains of Ethiopia. Two of the largest dams are those of the Gebel Awlia and Aswan reservoirs. The Gebel Awlia reservoir can hold 2,000 million cubic meters of water, and the famous Aswan reservoir holds twice this amount.

In its upper reaches the Nile has many tributaries, of which the largest is the Blue Nile.

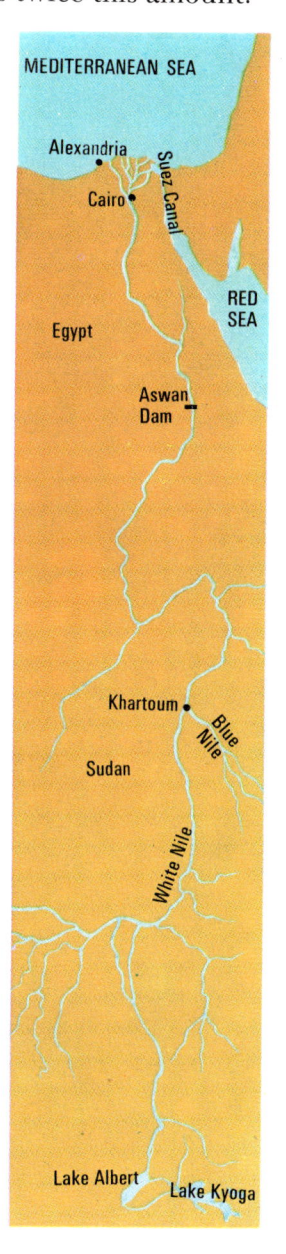

Left: Falls on the Blue Nile.

There is also a great dam across the Blue Nile at the village of Makwar, near Sennar, in the Sudan. This was built as part of a scheme for irrigating over a thousand square miles of land in the province of Gezira.

Besides irrigation, the Nile is also used by trading boats to and from Cairo, the capital, which is situated at the head of the delta. Above Aswan there are many shallows and rapids in the river.

Alexandria, where Nelson fought the Battle of the Nile against the French Fleet in 1798, is situated at the west of the Delta. At the east of the Delta is Port Said, which is on the northern entrance of the Suez Canal.

Nitrogen is a colorless, tasteless gas. It is the chemical element, symbol N. It is found in the air, and the Earth's atmosphere is nearly four-fifths nitrogen. Chemically, nitrogen is *inert*—that is, it does not readily take part in chemical reactions. For instance, it does not burn, nor will it support combustion.

Nitrogen is essential to life in plants and animals. It is found in protoplasm (the material in cells) and in proteins, which consist mainly of nitrogen-containing compounds called amino-acids. Plants get their nitrogen from compounds in the soil. These, in turn, get their nitrogen from the air or from fertilizers and decaying matter. Animals get their nitrogen by eating plants or by eating other animals. The way in which nitrogen passes from the soil to plants and animals and then back to the soil again is an important part of the balance of nature called the *nitrogen cycle*.

Animals also breathe in nitrogen. But it is not absorbed by the lungs and is breathed out again. Nitrogen is extracted from air for industrial use by cooling the air until it liquifies. The liquid air so formed is separated into its components, oxygen and nitrogen. Nitrogen also occurs in mineral deposits of nitrates in South America and Europe. It is used for making ammonia, fertilizers, explosives and plastics. Other nitrogen compounds are used as drugs.

Left: Nitrogen encourages rapid plant growth. It is taken in through the roots mainly as nitrate dissolved in the soil water. The plant on the left has been starved of nitrogen.

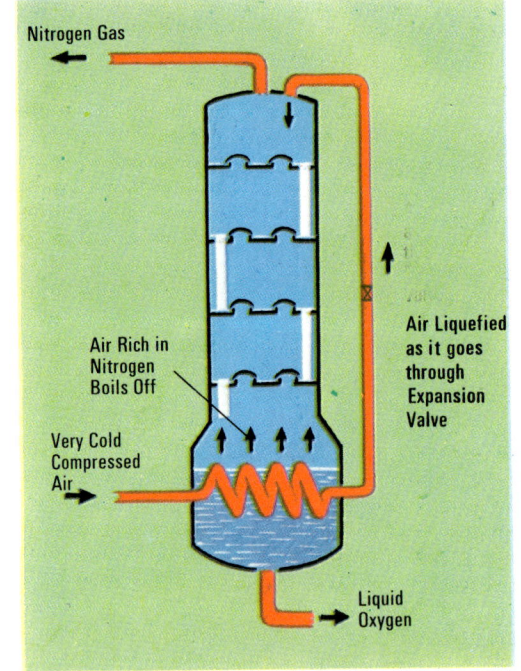

A simplified rectification column for separating oxygen and nitrogen. When liquid air comes into contact with cool gaseous air, nitrogen gas tends to boil off, while oxygen collects in the liquid. Almost pure nitrogen gas can be taken from the top of the column, while liquid oxygen can be removed from the base.

Nixon, Richard Milhous (1913-   ), a Republican, became the 37th president of the United States in 1969. In 1968, in one of the closest American presidential elections ever held, he defeated the Democrat, Hubert Humphrey. The most difficult problem inherited by President Nixon was the continuing war in Vietnam. Other issues that concerned many people included the civil rights movement, student protest and the unrest in many American cities.

Richard Nixon was born in the village of Yorba Linda, California. He was educated at Whittier College and Duke Law School and graduated third in his class in 1937. In 1940, Nixon married Thelma Patricia Ryan and they had two daughters, Patricia, born in 1946, and Julie, born in 1948. Nixon served with the navy from 1942 until 1946, and he was stationed in the South Pacific. His political career began in 1946 when he was elected to the House of Representatives by the voters of his home congressional district, and he was re-elected two years later.

Nixon first won fame for his work on the Committee on Un-American Activities. In 1948, Alger Hiss, a former State Department official, was charged with giving information to Communist agents. Nixon pressed the case against Hiss, although many others wanted the case to be dropped. Hiss was finally tried for perjury for denying the charges against him, and in 1950 he was sentenced to five years in prison.

In 1950, in California, Nixon defeated the Democrat, Helen Gahagan Douglas, in the election for U.S. Senator. In 1952, only six years after entering politics, Nixon was a national figure and he was chosen as running mate to General Dwight D. Eisenhower at the Republican Convention. Two months after the convention, Nixon was accused of having illegally used funds provided for his political expenses by a group of rich Californians. Nixon successfully defended himself against this charge.

From 1953 to 1961, Nixon served as vice president under President Eisenhower. Nixon was better known and more active than most earlier vice presidents. Because of Eisenhower's illnesses, Nixon had to stand in for the president on

Richard Nixon, 37th president of the United States, giving his first State of the Union address in January, 1970.

Richard Nixon greets astronauts Haise, Lovell and Swigert after presenting them with the Medal of Freedom on their safe return from the near-disaster of the Apollo 13 spacecraft flight to the moon in April 1970. Though the mission failed, the astronauts' safe return was a triumph for American technology.

several occasions. He also made many journeys around the world on good will tours on behalf of the president.

In 1960, Nixon was chosen as the Republican presidential candidate to succeed President Eisenhower. In a closely fought contest, Nixon was narrowly defeated by John F. Kennedy. After another electoral defeat in 1962, for the governorship of California, Nixon announced his retirement from politics. He then became a successful New York lawyer. In 1964, he supported Senator Barry Goldwater, the Republican candidate for president.

In 1968, however, Nixon returned to politics. He easily won the Republican presidential nomination, and in the election he defeated Hubert Humphrey and became president. Spiro Agnew became his vice president (see Agnew, Spiro).

Nkrumah, Kwame (1909-   ), was the first prime minister of the West African country of Ghana. He first became prime minister in 1952, when the country was still a British colony, the Gold Coast. Under his leadership, the country gained independence in 1957, and was renamed Ghana, the name of an ancient West African nation. (See Negro history.)

Nkrumah continued as prime minister of Ghana until 1960, when the country became a republic and Nkrumah its first president. Ghana made much progress, and Nkrumah also worked hard to develop *Pan-Africanism*—that is, united political action by all African peoples. But in Ghana itself he aroused much opposition by setting up a one-party state and imprisoning opposition leaders. Many people also thought his government was corrupt. Finally, in 1966, the army overthrew Nkrumah's government. He then settled in Guinea.

Nkrumah was born in Ankroful, Gold Coast, and educated in the United States and in England. He returned home in 1947, to lead the struggle for independence.

Kwame Nkrumah led Ghana (formerly Gold Coast) to independence in 1957.

Nobel, Alfred Bernhard (1833-1896), was a Swedish chemist and inventor. He is most famous for the discovery of dynamite and for establishing the annual Nobel prizes.

Nobel's father was a manufacturer of nitroglycerine. Many accidents took place during the handling of this highly dan-

Alfred Nobel aged thirty. He became one of the richest men of his day, but died a lonely and unhappy man.

gerous explosive, and Nobel was determined to find a way of making it safe. Eventually, by mixing the nitroglycerine with an absorbent substance called *Kieselguhr*, Nobel made a manageable explosive which he called *dynamite*. He also invented a blasting jelly and a smokeless gunpowder. Soon his factories sprang up all over the world.

But the knowledge that his inventions were being used for such violent acts as killing and destruction, rather than the peaceful purposes he had hoped for, weighed heavily on Nobel's conscience. In his will, Nobel set aside a large sum of money to be used for awarding annual prizes for outstanding achievements in several different fields. Nobel chose the fields of chemistry, physics, medicine or physiology, literature, and the advancement of peace. These prizes are highly esteemed as well as being financially valuable, and were first awarded in 1901.

Nomads are people who wander from place to place and have no permanent home. They usually travel within certain general areas according to the seasons and the supply of food. Hunting nomads, such as the pygmies of Africa and Asia, follow the animals that they kill to eat. Pastoral nomads, such as the Bedouins of Arabia, drive their herds of camels, goats, sheep and horses from one patch of grazing land to another. There is not enough vegetation to set up permanent farms.

Nomads generally live in tents or some equally simple type of shelter, and carry few belongings with them.

Norse myths The early Scandinavian peoples, who lived in the countries now called Sweden, Denmark, Norway and Iceland, invented a series of tales about the formation of the Earth and the activities of the gods and goddesses they believed in. These tales, which make up the Norse mythology, are contained in large collections, known as the *Eddas*.

According to the *Eddas*, before the Earth was formed, there were only two vague divisions of the Universe—a world of mist and a world of light. Fountains in the world of mist froze into ice. Warm winds from the other world melted some of the ice to vapor. From this vapor, so the story goes, sprang the giant Ymir and his children. Later, a god was created. He married a giant and they had three children: Odin, Vili and Ve. The legends relate how these three killed Ymir and created from his body the homes of the gods, the giants, and man, and a region of darkness where the dead who had not died in battle were forced to dwell.

Odin became chief among the gods, and was said to inhabit a magnificent palace, Valhalla. There he sat with two ravens perched on his shoulders.

The Norsemen had a demon god,

Nomads generally live in tents to enable them to move about freely.

called Loki. Many stories tell of his treachery. Balder, son of Odin, was handsome, wise and popular. His mother, Frigga, made all living and non-living things swear never to harm Balder. But Loki found out that Frigga had forgotten to ask one plant—the mistletoe—to spare Balder. He tricked Hod, the blind god of night, into killing Balder by throwing a piece of mistletoe at him.

The death of Balder was the beginning of the end. Loki led the giants and demons in a gigantic war against the gods. One by one the gods perished, even Odin and Thor. The end of the gods brought the doom of mankind. Earth, sky, stars and all things collapsed into the dark nothingness from which everything had come.

North America is the third largest of the world's continents and occupies nearly a fifth of the Earth's land area. Only Asia and Africa are larger. Its physical limits are Panama in the south, and Alaska and Greenland in the north. The northern four-fifths of the continent are occupied by Canada and the United States, while the remainder is made up of Mexico and Central America. There are also a large number of islands, the most important of which are the Caribbean Islands and Greenland, the world's largest.

North America has an area of 9,635,000 square miles. It is almost as wide as it is long: from north to south it stretches some 4,500 miles, and from east to west about 4,000 miles. It has a population of 295,600,000.

Its land regions are fairly well marked. The Lawrentian region is an area of low-lying rocky land that stretches around Hudson Bay. It extends from the Arctic Ocean in the north to Labrador in the east. Much of it is unexplored forest, well watered with icy lakes and streams.

The Appalachian region consists of a range of mountains running southwestward from Quebec in Canada to Alabama in southeastern United States. The Appalachians include the Allegheny plateau and other mountain ranges.

In the south of the continent, bordering the Gulf of Mexico and the Atlantic Ocean, there are flat coastal plains. Vast areas of these plains are swampy.

To the west lie the great Western Highlands. They are called the Cordilleras in Central America, and the Rocky Mountains in the rest of the continent. They stretch from Alaska to Central America. The highest peak in North America is Mt McKinley (20,320 ft), in Alaska. In the Colorado Rockies alone there are 55 peaks that reach 14,000 feet or more. Running parallel to the Rockies are the Coast and Cascade ranges, and the Sierra Nevada. They border a narrow, fertile, coastal strip along the shores of the Pacific.

The Great Plains form a 1,500-mile wide belt, including part of central and northern Canada and the interior of the United States. These are great grazing and grain-growing lands.

Rivers flow westward to the west of the Rockies, and eastward, southward, and northward on the eastern side of the mountains. Westward-flowing rivers, such as the Yukon, Snake, and Colorado are generally swift torrents. The Missouri-Mississippi river system is 3,700 miles long, one of the longest in the world. The St Lawrence flows eastward and connects the Great Lakes with the Atlantic.

The Great Lakes, on the borders of Canada and the United States, are an important group of lakes. They are lakes Superior, Michigan, Huron, Erie and Ontario. The best known falls are the Niagara Falls, which are famed for their striking scenery.

The climate in the far south is always warm, and in the far north it is always cold. Most of the continent has warm summers and cold winters. Rainfall is heavy (up to 140 inches a year) on the western slopes of the Rockies; but in the desert regions there may be only about 1½ inches of rain a year.

North America is still very rich in animal life, but as the population increases and spreads, the wildlife is rapidly disappearing from the continent. A hundred years ago the plains were filled with enormous herds of bison. Today, only a few herds remain, carefully protected in game preserves. Nevertheless, the woods of central and eastern North America still hold black bears, deer, muskrats, porcupines and beavers. The Rockies are the home of eagles, grizzly bears, elk, and moose. In the far north are found some of the most valuable fur-bearing animals, including Arctic foxes, fur seals and polar bears. Tropical creatures

Contrasting North American landscapes

Above: Not all of Alaska is a frozen waste. In some places quick-growing crops can be produced during the short summers.
Left: The Potomac River divides Virginia from Maryland, and flows out into Chesapeake Bay.
Below: Elephant Rock in the Valley of Fire State Park, Nevada. Much of the southern and central part of North America is desert or semi-arid country. In these areas the forces of erosion sometimes carve rock into fantastic shapes.

ARCTIC OCEAN
GREENLAND
HUDSON BAY
PACIFIC OCEAN
CANADA
Edmonton
Calgary
Regina
Winnipeg
Vancouver
Victoria
Seattle
Portland
St. John's
St. Lawrence
Quebec
Halifax
Montreal
Ottawa
Toronto
ATLANTIC OCEAN
Duluth
Missouri
UNITED STATES
ROCKY MOUNTAINS
Minneapolis
Milwaukee
Detroit
Buffalo
Boston
Salt Lake City
Platte
Omaha
Des Moines
Chicago
Cleveland
New York
Philadelphia
Pittsburgh
MOUNTAINS
San Francisco
Denver
Indianapolis
Baltimore
Washington
Colorado
Kansas City
St. Louis
Cincinnati
Los Angeles
Arkansas
Ohio
Richmond
Norfolk
San Diego
Wichita
APPALACHIAN
Memphis
Little Rock
Oklahoma City
Atlanta
El Paso
Birmingham
Fort Worth
Dallas
Rio Grande
Mississippi
Savannah
Jacksonville
New Orleans
San Antonio
Houston
Corpus Christi
Miami
GULF OF MEXICO
MEXICO
Havana
CUBA
DOMINICAN REPUBLIC
PUERTO RICO
HAITI
Mexico City
Veracruz
JAMAICA
BRITISH HONDURAS
GUATEMALA
CARIBBEAN SEA
HONDURAS
NICARAGUA
COSTA RICA
PANAMA
60°N
20°N
140°W
100°W
60°W
Cool Coniferous Forest
Temperate Forest
Tropical Forest
Equatorial Rain Forest
Grass
Temperate Desert
Savanna
Tundra Icecaps
Hot Desert
Mountain Vegetation
0 200 400 600 800 1000
Scale in Miles

January Temperatures

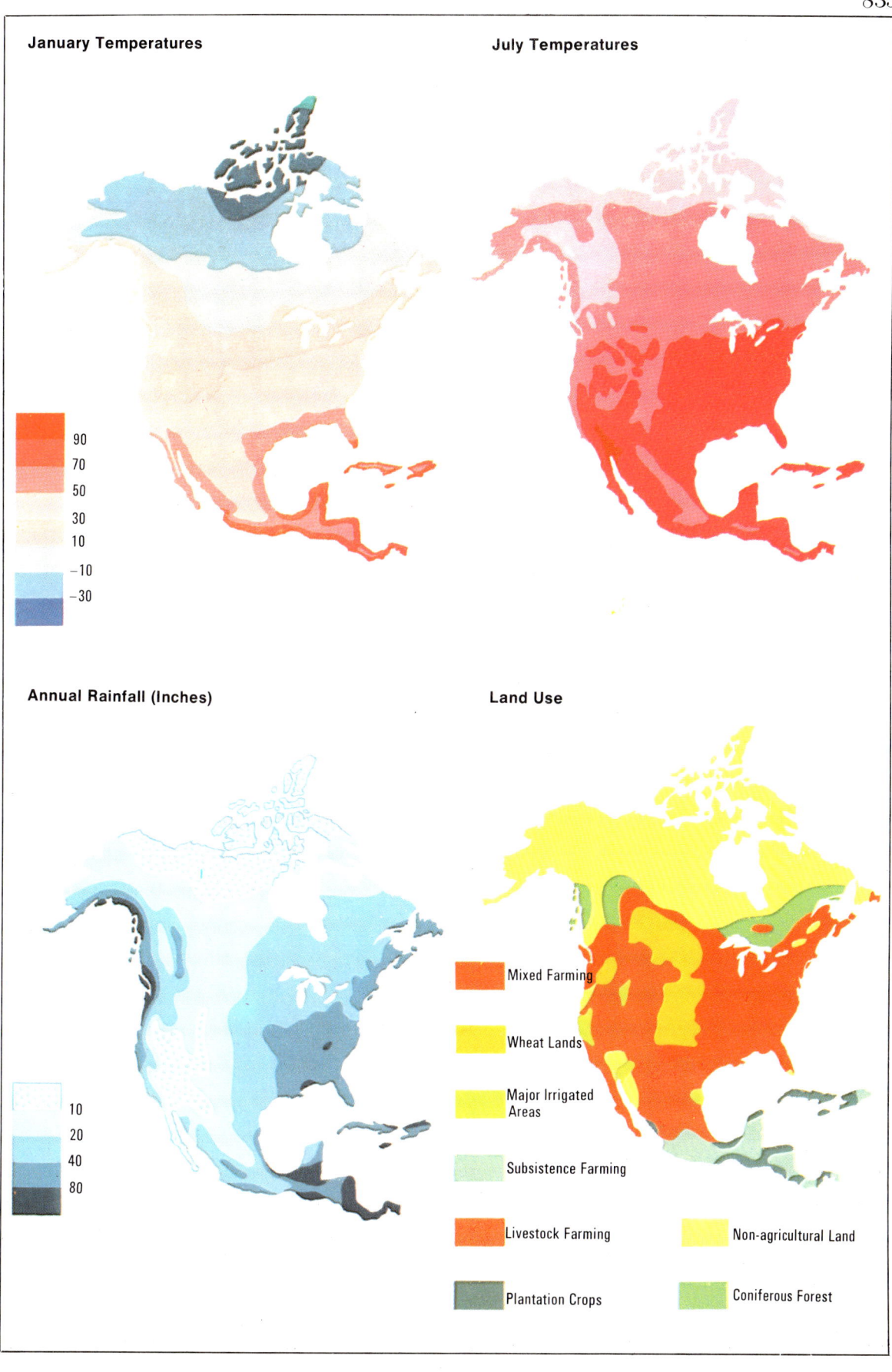

July Temperatures

90
70
50
30
10
−10
−30

Annual Rainfall (Inches)

10
20
40
80

Land Use

- Mixed Farming
- Wheat Lands
- Major Irrigated Areas
- Subsistence Farming
- Livestock Farming
- Non-agricultural Land
- Plantation Crops
- Coniferous Forest

836

NORTH AMERICA
Plants and Animals

NORTH AMERICA
Minerals

- Coal
- Natural Gas
- Petroleum
- Uranium
- Cobalt
- Iron Ore
- Molybdenum
- Nickel
- Vanadium
- Tungsten
- Asbestos
- Silver
- Bauxite
- Gold
- Copper
- Mercury
- Potash
- Mica
- Phosphates
- Lead
- Platinum
- Sulphur
- Titanium
- Zinc

838
NORTH AMERICA
Exploration

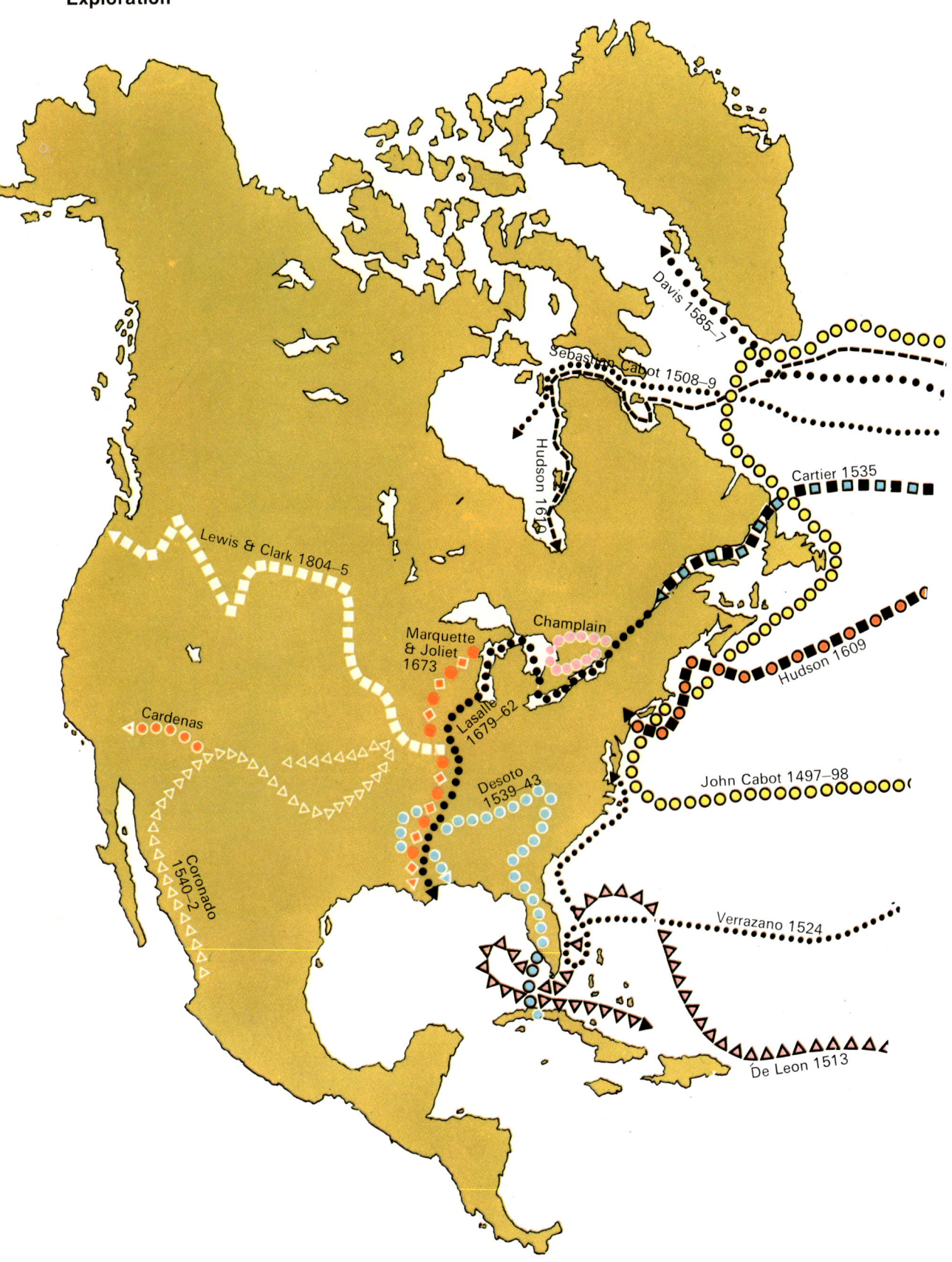

such as alligators, monkeys, jaguars, anteaters, armadillos and a host of colorful birds inhabit Central America.

North America's plant life varies from the mosses and lichens that survive in the coldest regions of the Arctic, to the desert cactus of the waterless areas of the southwest. Trees include the redwoods and sequoias of California (the largest trees in the world), maples (whose leaf is the emblem of Canada) and tropical palms. Canada has enormous forests of fir, spruce and pine. The vast grasslands of the Great Plains feed herds of sheep and cattle.

North American agriculture is strikingly uneven. In the United States and Canada there are millions of acres of fertile land, and the yield per acre is constantly increasing because farmers use the latest equipment and methods. Canada exports more than half its wheat harvest to other countries. But in the Latin American countries of the continent the land is so poor and farming methods and machinery so out-of-date that there is barely enough food produced to feed the population. Coffee, bananas and sugar are the chief crops of most of the Central American countries.

North America has some of the world's richest deposits of minerals. The most important are coal, petroleum, gold, iron, nickel, silver, lead, zinc and copper. Both Canada and the United States are among the leading industrial nations of the world, with large manufacturing

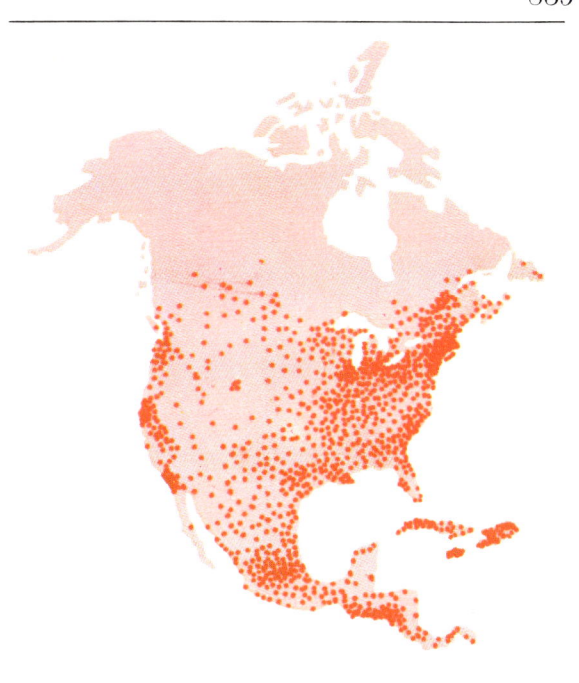

A map showing the distribution of population in North America.

COUNTRIES OF NORTH AMERICA

Country	Area (sq. mi.)	Population	Capital
Canada	3,851,809	20,376,000	Ottawa
Costa Rica	19,575	1,453,000	San José
Cuba	44,218	7,598,000	Havana
Dominican Republic	18,816	3,657,000	Santo Domingo
El Salvador	8,260	2,908,000	San Salvador
Guatemala	42,042	4,412,000	Guatemala
Haiti	10,714	4,706,000	Port-au-Prince
Honduras	43,277	2,223,000	Tegucigalpa
Jamaica	4,232	1,732,000	Kingston
Mexico	761,602	42,244,000	Mexico City
Nicaragua	57,143	1,697,000	Managua
Panama	29,209	1,270,000	Panama
Trinidad and Tobago	1,980	990,000	Port-of-Spain
United States (excluding Hawaii)	3,669,209	203,184,772	Washington D.C.

TERRITORIES OF NORTH AMERICA

Territory	Area (sq. mi.)	Population	Capital	Status
Bahamas	4,400	122,000	Nassau	British colony
Bermuda	21	46,000	Hamilton	British colony
Greenland	840,001	37,000	Godthaab	County of Denmark
Guadeloupe	687	310,000	Basse-Terre	Overseas department of France
Honduras, British	8,867	107,000	Belize	British colony
Martinique	425	319,000	Fort-de-France	Overseas department of France
Netherlands Antilles	371	209,000	Willemstad	Self-governing member of the Kingdom of The Netherlands
Panama Canal Zone	553	47,000	Balboa Heights	U.S. leasehold from Panama
Puerto Rico	3,435	2,742,000	San Juan	U.S. commonwealth
Saint Pierre and Miquelon	93	5,000	Saint Pierre	French overseas territory
Virgin Islands (British)	59	8,000	Road Town	British colony
Virgin Islands (U.S.)	132	63,000	Charlotte Amalie	U.S. territory

This picture of a typical group of American factory workers shows how people of many different ethnic groups have chosen to settle in North America.

centers in many places. But the Latin American countries import a large quantity of their manufactured goods, because local industries cannot supply all the country's needs.

Most of the people in the Latin American countries of the continent speak Spanish, but in the United States and Canada, English (with some French in Canada) is the main language.

Some of the world's greatest cities are located in North America. The largest Canadian cities are Montreal, Toronto and Vancouver. In the United States, New York City, Los Angeles, Chicago, Philadelphia, Detroit and Houston are the main population centers, each with more than a million people. In the Latin American countries Mexico City and Havana, in Cuba, are the largest cities.

The first European explorers reached North America nearly 500 years ago. The wild region they found was inhabited by Indians who are believed to have come originally from Asia. They probably traveled from Asia during the Ice Age, about 20,000 years ago. During that time the sea level was much lower than it is today and there was probably a land link between the North American and Asian continents. The North American Indians have certain similarities to the Mongols. The Aztec and Maya Indians of Mexico developed high standards of civilization, but the northern Indians reached a far less advanced level.

In the far north the Eskimos arrived from Asia about 2,000 years ago. Most inhabitants of the continent have European ancestors, but about a tenth of the people are Negroes, descendants of slaves brought from Africa to North America between the 1600's and the early 1800's.